PRAISE FOR
HELP! MY TODDLER CAME WITHOUT INSTRUCTIONS!

Once again, Blythe uses her unique sense of humor to teach parents how to manage their offspring so that the experience is wonderful and happy for parents and child.

—Sandy Adler, Scottsdale, AZ

After producing Blythe's radio shows for over three years on Toginet Radio, I feel this is a MUST read for any parent or grandparent. Blythe's expertise and knowledge into what goes on in these "little minds" is amazing! She provides wonderful and tangible tips, not to mention how she breaks it down into step-by-step instructions! What a great gift to give to someone at a baby shower!

—Jill Martin, Lindale, TX

Blythe Lipman is an amazingly talented toddler expert, and her book is invaluable! The book is full of wonderful, helpful, sanity saving tips and hints and is infused with Blythe's terrific sense of humor. If you have a toddler, you have to have this book!

—Irma M. Ross, LPC, NCC, Norwalk, CT

I remember being a brand-new mother and being so nervous. I set the timer and tried to schedule my day with this brand-new baby. I was baffled that my baby just did not want to comply with that timer! How I wish I had Blythe in my corner then! Blythe's first book, *Help! My Baby Came Without Instructions,* is the perfect balance of common sense and practical answers for just about anything a new mother could be faced with. Now, when baby becomes a toddler, new parents can rely on her second book, *Help! My Toddler Came Without Instructions,* with its practical tips, safety guidelines, smart ways to engage baby and help those years between ages one and four be precious, enjoyable, and the best foundation for your baby's development.

—Robin Boyd, Hooksett, NH

The early years of children's development are critical and parents really are the first teachers. Schools just build on the learning that parents have already started. As a kindergarten teacher who has shared the first year at school with over a thousand little ones, I know from experience the difference that parents make. For all the tests your little ones will come up with, get the answers here in *Help! My Toddler Came Without Instructions.*

—Mrs. Allisen, Nanaimo, BC, Canada

While there are many parenting books on the market, this one stands alone. It gives parents immediate solutions to solve their common toddler issues when they occur. Each tip is fast, easy, and proven to work. So when your little one is screaming at the top of his lungs or refuses to eat his dinner,

Help! My Toddler Came Without Instructions will tell you just what to do. It's the best sanity insurance you'll ever buy!

—Dr. Gary A. Witt, Scottsdale, AZ

Blythe has created a great tool to help parents transition from managing a baby to the new and somewhat challenging experiences of dealing with a toddler. This simple guide provides tips that work and work quickly. It's a must-have on your bookshelf for easy access in times of emergency!

—Kelly Damron, Phoenix, AZ,
author of *Tiny Toes: A Couple's Journey through Infertility, Prematurity, and Depression*

Toddlers are tough but Blythe Lipman shows that with a little elbow grease and ingenuity, they can be a breeze! Simple steps in a quick, fun, and easy-to-read format make this instruction manual one you'll keep close by for taming your toddler. Pick up a copy for yourself and a friend!

—M. B. Sanok,
Executive Editor of *South Jersey MOM* magazine and blogger for Jersey Moms Blog

You can ask my mom about anything when it comes to toddlers and I am living proof! I have her to thank for becoming who I am today. She always set such great examples and continues to do so! Every parent with a toddler needs to have this book in their library. Her wonderful expertise and easy tips can turn a tantrum into a learning experience in minutes. I have seen it with my own eyes.

—Andrew Lipman, son, Scottsdale, AZ

This book is outstanding! I have raised three children and the one thing I like about Blythe's advice is how candid it is. She knows what works because she has been there. She has an authentic, flexible approach that makes sense and fits the modern family. Thanks, Blythe, for all your great tips and strategies!

—Julianna Lyddon, Paradise Valley, AZ

Help! My Toddler Came Without Instructions is written in a concise, yet friendly format that Lipman is known for. If there was ever a book that parents of toddlers should have, this is it!

—Shannon Duffy, Palm Springs, CA
coauthor, *The Couple's Guide to Pregnancy & Beyond*

When I was a little girl, my mom always had a baby or toddler in her care. The one thing I can remember is that they were always happy! She knew just what they needed and their tears were few and far between. I am so proud of her and also lucky that she's my mom! I learned so much from her. "Thanks, Mom!"

—Lindsay Lipman, daughter, Glendale, AZ

I was so excited to see that Blythe Lipman wrote another book in her "Help" series. I wouldn't have survived those first few years as a new parent without *Help! My Baby Came Without Instructions*. And now that my little one has just entered the "terrible two's," *Help! My Toddler Came Without Instructions* is my toddler bible!

—Ali W., Maui, HI

Help! My Toddler Came Without Instructions is the perfect follow-up to Blythe Lipman's first book about babies. She has over thirty years of experience and many secrets for a happier child. With each age comes a new set of questions and challenges. Blythe's advice and suggestions are useful but written with a great sense of humor. And we all need to laugh while raising these little people. This is my favorite gift to give new parents.

—Maureen Lipson, Paradise Valley, AZ

I thought I would scream if my toddler put her finger in her nose one more time! But while all the parenting books say don't draw attention to these issues with your toddler, *Help! My Toddler Came Without Instructions* says that and so much more. Her expertise and real-life tips are the best and help immediately! It's my favorite new gift for all my friends with toddlers.

—Jeanine J., Boulder, CO

I truly thought the baby years were a challenge and it would get easier as my little one got older and slept through the night. No one prepared me for tantrums, meal battles, separation anxiety, and trying to find time for me and for my marriage. *Help! My Toddler Came Without Instructions* showed me it can be done and with very few tears (mine or my toddler's!). Can't wait for Blythe's next book in the series.

—Jacqueline F., Paris, France

HELP!
MY TODDLER
CAME WITHOUT
INSTRUCTIONS

HELP!
MY TODDLER
CAME WITHOUT
INSTRUCTIONS

Practical Tips for Parenting a Happy One, Two, Three and Four Year Old

BY BLYTHE LIPMAN

ViVa
EDITIONS

Published in the United States by Viva Editions, an imprint of Cleis Press, Inc., 2246 Sixth Street, Berkeley, California 94710.

Printed in the United States.
Cover design: Scott Idleman/Blink
Cover photograph: Photodisc
Text design and illustrations: Frank Wiedemann
First Edition.
10 9 8 7 6 5 4 3 2 1

Trade paper ISBN: 978-1-57344-954-0
E-book ISBN: 978-1-936740-48-2

Library of Congress Cataloging-in-Publication Data

Lipman, Blythe.
 Help! My toddler came without instructions : practical tips for parenting a happy one, two, three and four year old / Blythe Lipman. -- First edition.
    pages cm.
 ISBN 978-1-57344-954-0 (pbk. : alk. paper)
 1. Toddlers--Care. 2. Child rearing. 3. Parenting. I. Title.
 HQ774.5.L57 2013
 649'.1--dc23
                        2013000741

To my children...
Lindsay and Andrew,
you truly make my heart smile.

TABLE OF CONTENTS

ACKNOWLEDGMENTS

I am truly blessed to have so many wonderful people in my life that helped this book go from conception to delivery. Sending big "thank you hugs" from the bottom of my heart! I will be forever grateful to all of you.

To Gary, for your wonderful words of wisdom, for those Friday night pizza and wine dinners at Redendo's, for your understanding and support, and knowing when to give me space and when to be there when my words got stuck. But thank you, most of all, for your never-ending faith in me.

Lindsay and Andrew, my wonderful children. Reminiscing about your toddler years is always so much fun. Sometimes laughing so hard that I almost fell off the chair remembering some of the things I did and how scared I was thinking I would make a mistake as your mom, added so much to this book. Seeing you now, my wonderful grown-up and responsible, fun-loving children truly makes my heart smile.

Jo, Adrienne, Sandy, Sylvia, Lynn, Maureen, my Group, my Girl-friends, my happy hour buddies, my ladies to lunch with, my conscience, and my biggest fans. You were always there, listening, debating, contrib-uting, understanding, meeting me for coffee, setting up a movie day, a quick lunch, a happy hour, a phone call long or short, and understanding when I just had to say "no." I am truly blessed.

Irma and Sharon, my oldest and dearest friends, my favorite cheer-leaders, our days at Boston University may have been a few years ago, but as the saying goes, "We're not getting older, we're getting better!" And isn't that the truth! Your long-distance phone calls, emails, text messages, funny greeting cards, great suggestions, and never-ending patience deserve the biggest "thank you hug."

A radio host with my own show, me? Nah! But wait, I host *Baby and Toddler Instructions* on Toginet radio each week and love it! The things I've learned from all my wonderful guests has added a dimension to this book that would have never happened without the Toginet family: John, Jill, Keri, Ashley, Sabrina, Erik, J. Douglas Barker (Jdog), Bobby Bell, and all the wonderful radio hosts. Thank you for this wonderful opportunity each week to share my information and welcome my awesome guests to share theirs. You've all helped to make my book that much better. A special thank you to Robin Boyd, Carol McManus, and Josephine Geraci. Your stories, tips, honest opinions, insights, social media help, and friendship are such a joy.

And I would be remiss without sending a gigantic thank you to Beth and Lenny Wasserman. Spending many weekends as a young adolescent in your home taking care of my baby cousin, Pammy, playing "mommy" while you got to sleep late, speaks volumes. You thought you were getting the good end of the deal but I was truly the winner, knowing at eleven years old that caring for babies, toddlers, and their families was going to be my true destiny.

Help! My Toddler Came Without Instructions would never be in your hands without you, my wonderful toddler parents. You not only invited me into your homes, preschools, and daycare centers to share ideas and tips, and let me use your little miracles for my research and development, but you allowed me the honor of watching your toddlers blossom, grow, and strive for that independence as they reached each milestone.

And how could I ever write this book without my agent, June Clark, my publisher, Brenda Knight, and all the wonderful women at Viva Editions. Your confidence in me as an author has truly filled me with gratitude and made this book possible.

I am truly blessed to have you all in my life and could not be more grateful. Thank you from the bottom of my heart! I've won the lottery again!

FOREWORD

When my son George had just turned two, without any prompting by his Mom or myself, he picked up the telephone receiver to answer a mock call. George mumbled some beautiful nonsense to the non-caller with dramatic flair, took appropriate pauses, and laughed heartily every couple of phrases. For that moment, he was a "mini-me," dipping his toe into the next remarkable developmental stage in his life. I can still feel the ridiculous joy of that precious moment as I sit here and write. When your baby becomes a toddler, and you begin to witness shades of their personality beginning to reveal themselves, joy is inevitable. More importantly, George's own distinct features, all that is *just him*, came to the fore as well. Over the course of the toddler years, we have the privilege of witnessing a fresh new personality, funny, willful, and oddly wise, arising from the folds of soft newborn skin.

Of course, there are challenges in this new phase as well. Your toddler realizes the extent of his abilities for the first time. He can push your buttons. He knows "No!" He now possesses a discerning palate, and may whip unacceptable cuisine about the kitchen. He has remarkably little regard for either hygiene or heirlooms. He can attend, or ignore, at will. Suddenly, he's a force, and you are certain, all of this, will serve him well one day, in a boardroom, a courtroom, a classroom, with his own children.

But today, he may just exhaust you.

This is where a little guidance comes in handy. And in your hand you hold a reference that is clear, practical, comforting, funny, and wholly user-friendly. I encourage you to keep *Help! My Toddler Came Without Instructions* close, and refer to it often. The author, Blythe Lipman, is a consummate pro when it comes to parenting toddlers. Not only has she successfully raised her own children, but has served for many years as a baby and toddler expert and parenting consultant helping over a thousand families. Blythe's expertise is sought out by many radio, television, and print outlets and online. She is the host of her own weekly radio show called *Baby and Toddler Instructions* that has a national following. Blythe's social media information as well as her website, www.babyinstructions.com, provide wonderful tips, articles, and solutions that give parents the confidence they need to know they are doing a great job!

I talk a lot about availability in parenting. Based on my many years in clinical practice with children, parents, and families, I find that we parent best when we are fully available to our children, physically, intellectually, and emotionally. We are at our best when we keep our fears, judgments, and our own egos at bay. It's mighty work for any parent, and the toddler years present a particular set of challenges. *Help! My Toddler Came Without Instructions* addresses virtually all of them, and allows not only for available parenting, but the easy-to-use tips will make those sometimes trying toddler years a little easier. And trust me. You want to be there for every step, stumble, scream, goofy moment, pasta toss, and mock phone call!

I encourage you to drink in these years, and be fully available to them, as they are fleeting and magical. *Help! My Toddler Came Without Instructions* will help you enjoy every moment.

—John Duffy, MD

Dr. John Duffy, parenting and relationship expert, and author of *The Available Parent: Radical Optimism for Raising Teens and Tweens* (Viva Editions, 2011), writes a blog on the Huffington Post, and appears regularly on *The Steve Harvey Show* on NBC.

PREFACE

As a practicing pediatrician with forty years' experience, I was most pleased to hear that Blythe Lipman was publishing a sequel to her first book, *Help! My Baby Came Without Instructions*. This new book concentrates on ages one through four years, a most challenging time for children as well as their parents.

With many parents living long distances from their own families, grandmother is no longer nearby to help with the daily demands of raising a toddler, and also not available to lend advice directly when a new situation arises. Consulting the pediatrician for child-rearing concerns may not be feasible, given the demands on the doctor's time. Lengthy telephone conversations with the pediatrician or a nurse may not be as available as in the past.

As before, Blythe has drawn on her own vast experience as a mother and as a caregiver for many children in the community. She also consults experts in the field and searches the literature to add to her own experience. I have known her for over twenty years, and have been impressed by her common-sense approach to everyday parenting challenges.

This book is filled with charts, vignettes, and solid advice about problems that all parents encounter. There is also a much-needed chapter on keeping the parents' marriage thriving despite the stresses of raising children.

The chapters on discipline and toilet training are especially well written and most important.

I continue to recommend Blythe's book on infant care to new parents, and now will have this new volume to recommend to parents as their child enters toddlerhood.

—Alan B. Singer, MD
Phoenix, Arizona

INTRODUCTION

You did it—you got through that first year with your adorable, soft, cuddly, sweet-smelling, smiling, cooing, hungry, tired, gassy, screaming baby. And you thought that was tough. So who is this Cranky, Clingy, Picky, Screaming, Biting, Hitting, Non-listening, Rambunctious little being that is trying to rule your world? Your toddler, of course.

Ahh, toddlerhood, doesn't this just say it all?

Toddlerhood is about becoming independent. Once your little one is up and walking, she wants to try and do most things by herself. And toddlers know no boundaries. They think they can do anything! And that can sure make for a scary world in a parent's eyes.

The toddler stage starts around your child's first birthday and continues until they are four years old. In just one short year, they go from crawling to walking to running. And toddlers have unbelievable energy, which makes naptimes shorter and shorter.

And remember, toddlers live in the present. To them, yesterday is ancient history and tomorrow could mean next year. So those big events don't count as much as those special little moments which happen each day. And toddlers want Mommy and Daddy's undivided attention at all times!

But what do you do when your toddler asks the same questions over and over? What about when you are in a hurry to leave and she wants to show you how she dressed herself? And oh, those temper tantrums on the grocery store floor...so embarrassing! Where, when, and how do you set boundaries? Are you being too overprotective or too lenient? Yikes...where are the instructions?

They are right here, in your hand. *Help! My Toddler Came Without Instructions* is filled with pediatrician-approved, parent-tested, user-friendly tips to help make those toddler years a whole lot easier.

This book is simple to use; no cumbersome reading here. When a toddler issue arises, just go down the page and pick the solution that fits the problem. The thing to remember is one size doesn't fit all. Each toddler, parent, and family is wonderfully unique. And there is no right or wrong. What works for one family may not work for another. I have successfully used each and every tip in my book and know they can help.

The key to success during these sometimes challenging years is to be consistent. And we all know it's easier to give in because we don't want an argument, tantrum, or we're just too tired to say "no." Toddlers are "me"-centered. Life is all about them and they want immediate gratification. So letting them know the ground rules, and yes, you will have to repeat them over and over, makes life more manageable for everyone. Toddlers and transition do not always fit like a glove. But being a consistent parent will make everyone's life easier. Knowing the parameters and sticking to them pays off in the long and short run. And the tips in my book will help you accomplish this with ease.

I have taken care of infants, toddlers, and their families for over thirty-five years while using each and every tip in this book. And I have to tell you there is nothing that has brought me more joy than watching those little ones blossom and grow as they reached each milestone. Seeing a toddler's eyes light up with happiness as she successfully accomplished something new has truly made my heart smile.

Remember, imitation is the sincerest form of flattery and you are your toddler's number-one role model. Have fun watching your precious as she tackles each new task. Bask in her glory while you both enjoy the journey because in the blink of an eye, your pride and joy will be asking for the keys to the car!

Lastly, my use of "she" throughout the book is in no way gender-biased, but a merely a way to make reading consistent.

—Blythe Lipman

> "Enjoy the little things, for one day you may look back
> and realize they were the big things."
> —*Robert Brault*

THE TODDLER'S CREED

If I want it, IT'S MINE!

If I give it to you and change my mind later, IT'S MINE!

If I can take it away from you, IT'S MINE!

If it's mine it will never belong to anybody else, no matter what.

If we are building something together, all the pieces are mine!

If it looks just like mine, IT'S MINE!

If it breaks or needs putting away, IT'S YOURS!

—Dr. Burton L. White

TODDLERS GONE WILD!

Negative Behavior and Discipline

Your toddler is happily playing with blocks with her big sister and wham…
she decides to throw a block at her. You tell her to stop, but to no avail,
another block goes hurling across the room and hits big sister right in the
head, ouch!

The grand test of parenting is how well *you* handle your temper when
your toddler just won't listen. Your personal reserve of inner discipline
is your grand test. Limits are limits and you know what is dangerous and
what is not. It is your job as a parent to teach your toddler about acceptable

behavior. Being able to calmly say "no" for the twentieth time is a challenge for any parent. Consistency is the key. "No" means "No" whether it is the first time or the hundredth time.

The following tips should help to keep the peace:

Talk to your mate about discipline during the baby years. Make sure you are both on the same page. There is nothing more confusing to a toddler than inconsistency. Toddlers are very smart and will quickly learn who the easy one is!

If your mate uses a method you don't agree with, go into another room to discuss it; never in front of your toddler. And don't interfere and take your toddler out of time-out if daddy has just put her in there. Undermining your mate does not make for a good role model.

I Was So Mad by Mercer Mayer is a great book to read if your toddler has a difficult time listening.

Routine, Routine, Routine! Having a consistent daily routine will make things easier all around. Your toddler will know what's coming next and be prepared.

Use a kitchen timer to give a ten-minute warning when a transition is about to happen. Let your toddler help set the timer and give her some control. Watching her complete a task by the time the bell rings and seeing her eyes light up is the perfect reward.

Give your toddler a choice when you want her to do something. It will not only make her feel like a big girl but teaches her to think for herself. For example: "Do you want to pick up your toys before or after your bath?" It's also great for her self-esteem.

Offer her limited and easy choices. It will make life simpler as she's learning to think for herself. "Do you want yogurt or cereal for breakfast or do you want to wear the pink or blue shirt?"

When your toddler is reluctant to choose, voice the one you would really prefer her to do last. Most times a toddler will pick the last one mentioned because it is what she heard last.

Offer choices *you* can live with and consistently stick to. Changing your mind only confuses your toddler.

Decide ahead of time which things are worth fighting over. Safety issues, naptimes, and bedtimes are not negotiable.

Repeat your request twice and remind your toddler what the consequence will be if she doesn't listen. Then follow through even if you are tired. "If you throw a block again, you are going to have a time-out." Short and sweet does the trick.

If you tell your child to do something and she keeps asking you why, after three clear explanations from you ask her to tell *you* why.

Redirect an unwanted behavior by suggesting another activity. "Can you draw a picture for me? Do you want to play with this red truck? I know you love the color red!" Distraction works great with most toddlers.

Always compliment the positive and don't draw attention to the negative. "You are drawing such a pretty picture."

If you are going to use time-outs, state very clearly why they will happen and follow through each time an unacceptable behavior is repeated.

Walk your toddler over to the time-out area. Don't expect her to put herself in time-out.

Have a time-out in a boring place with no toys or playmates nearby, such as the stairs. Do not use your child's bedroom for time-outs or you will teach her to associate it with punishment. (S. Debroff, p. 217)

If your toddler keeps coming out of time-out, gently take her back to the area and resist repeating what she did. You may have to take her back more than a few times. Try to be patient as this is a perfect teaching opportunity.

When time-out is over, if she needs to apologize to big sister or another playmate, do it immediately and then let it go. Action speaks louder than words.

A toy time-out can be your savior when your toddler is being destructive with her toys. Label a box with "Toy Time-out." Put the toys in the box for the rest of the day. Even though your toddler may forget about it and move on to play with another, she will remember when you give it back the next time. Toddlers have great memories.

Try to rotate your toddler's toys every few months. Old becomes new again and your toddler will love it!

If your toddler keeps repeating the same bad behavior, make a sticker chart. And don't make it too complicated. Getting five stickers earns a reward. And keep the rewards simple: ice cream, new crayons, or watching

Even very young children have bewilderingly good memories. Twenty years ago, a study on memories of Walt Disney World—the *ne plus ultra* memorable experience—surprised everyone involved: Children who'd been at Disney when they were only three years old could recount detailed memories of it eighteen months later. Evidence has piled up ever since. A just-published paper on long-term recall found that a twenty-seven-month-old child who'd seen a "magic shrinking machine" remembered the experience some six years later. (www.slate.com/ a division of *The Washington Post*)

a special video with mommy or daddy.

If you find your toddler constantly acting out during playtime, think about doing some rearranging. Take a good look around the room. Are there too many toys, too many chairs, and not enough room for play? Enlist your little one's help to make the room more toddler-friendly. Let her choose some toys to be put away, move a chair, or help with any other part of making the playroom new and improved. Being a part of the process is so important and change can be so much fun!

Acknowledge your toddler's feelings when your child is doing an unacceptable behavior; she wants to be heard. Get down to her level, look into those little eyes, and say, "I know you want to play at the park longer, but it's time to go eat lunch." A little understanding and empathy goes a long way when she is frustrated. We all like validation.

It's not necessary to give a long-winded explanation when you want

One mom said when her four-year-old toddler didn't want to leave the park, she would acknowledge her feelings, give her a hug then take her by the hand and say, "Let's see how many green things we can find on our way home."

your toddler to do something. "Stop hitting your sister, it hurts," is enough.

Make sure the punishment fits the crime. As Dr. Bill Sears says, "When you use time-outs, one minute per the age of the child works best. Keeping a two-year-old in time-out for five minutes is not necessary."

When disciplining your toddler, try not to use "you" words. Positive reinforcement works so much better for self-esteem. The wrong way: "You are a bad girl when you don't put your toys away." A better way: "I like it when you put your toys away."

Try your best to stay calm when disciplining your toddler. If you lose your cool it's all over. Toddlers are very smart!

There may be times when your toddler gets into a harmful situation and there is no time for you to react in a calm manner. It's okay. Once she is out of harm's way and you've calmed down inside, give

To get my kids to behave I make the house or something else the authority. I'll say, "In this house, children under three wear bibs when eating." You can't really argue with the house. (S. Debroff, p. 219)

her a big hug and say, "Mommy gets scared when you let go of her hand in the parking lot." Again, there is no need for long explanations.

If your toddler answers you with negative words, listen to yourself. Do you use these words? Being a good role model is so important.

If you want to distract your toddler, take on another role, be grandma or grandpa or have your child be the mommy or daddy. It's fun and works great.

Tell your toddler stories about how you used to do things when you were a little girl. "My mommy used to put the toothpaste on my toothbrush just like I put on yours."

Use reverse psychology...this is good for a distraction and may bring on the giggles. "Don't you put your toys away. You're not allowed" always worked great when my children were toddlers.

When your toddler is really sad, challenge her with something fun—pretend to tickle her and say, "Don't you laugh!"

Sharing is not an easy concept for toddlers. Try using the words "take turns" instead of sharing. And again, use a kitchen timer. It's much easier for a toddler to understand "It's Lindsay's turn now and when the bell rings it will be your turn." The easier the concept the more success you will have.

When a toddler comes over for a playdate and it's time for her to leave, send home a special treat. It will make the good-byes much easier. A plate of cookies you baked during the visit or a special picture she colored are great mementos.

When your toddler won't let you change her pants, make it silly. Say, "Oh my, stinky pants, I wouldn't want to have those stinky pants, let's call daddy and ask him if he has stinky pants!" Most times making a toddler laugh is a good diversion and a great way to get cooperation.

Always leave extra time to get ready to go out. It may take more time than you think and unforeseen circumstances can always pop up when a toddler is involved. The more you push, the slower your toddler will move.

Just Shopping with Mom by Mercer Mayer is a great book to read before you go shopping with your toddler.

When taking your toddler to the grocery store with you, ask her to push the child-sized cart and help. Being mommy's big helper is the best!

Give your toddler some coupons, and when you go to the appropriate aisle, ask her to try to find the food from the picture on the coupon.

If you have a difficult time getting your toddler to do errands with you, promise a special treat before you go home. Maybe a trip to the park or to get some ice cream would be fun.

When your toddler is giving you a difficult time about doing errands with you, make up a fun game. Say, "While mommy is driving, we are going to look out the window and see how many red cars we can find."

Leave some wiggle room for your toddler to learn. You don't have to be a drill sergeant to teach your child right from wrong. As long as she is safe, give her a chance to figure things out for herself.

THE ABCS OF TODDLER CARE

The fundamental job of a toddler is to rule the universe.
—*Lawrence Kutner*

If you're going to reward your toddler for jobs well done, make sure to keep the rewards simple. A high-five, cheering, and hugs are just as great as an expensive toy. If you start out with the "big stuff," you're pretty much up the creek.
—*Jill M., Texas*

When our toddler was having a meltdown, we put him in his room, locked the door, and told him to call us when he was finished. We would hear him calling us almost immediately as he didn't want to miss the action outside his room.
—*Benjamin G., Maine*

The toddler craves independence, but he fears desertion.
—*Dorothy Corkville Briggs*

When my kids became wild and unruly, I used a nice, safe playpen. When they were finished, I climbed out.
—*Erma Bombeck*

CREATIVE STICKER CHART

It's always important to catch your toddler being good and reward her. One fun and effective way to acknowledge her is by using a creative sticker chart. Now you and your toddler can track good behavior together every day!

HOW IT WORKS

Draw a picture of your little one's favorite dessert. Include empty circles on your drawing and cover them with stickers when you notice good behavior. Be sure to place the sticker chart at your toddler's eye level so she can see it every day and to let her add the stickers herself. When the drawing is filled up with stickers, take your child out for a special night where she gets to pick a dessert of her choosing. This has been successful for reinforcing good behavior, focusing on good times, and creating happy memories.

OUCH, THAT HURT...

Toddlers and Aggressive Behavior

"If you hit your sister again you're going into time-out!" "Teeth are not for biting!" "No pushing!" "Please stop screaming!" Sound familiar? Once toddlerhood strikes, aggressive behavior could rear its ugly head. While toddlers want to be independent, everything is new and they don't know the ground rules yet. When they want something it's full speed ahead. Immediate gratification is the name of the game. They will hit, bite, push, pull, and do whatever it takes to get what they want with little regard for anyone or anything else. It's our job as parents to teach them acceptable behavior, patience, and respect. While it's not always an easy task, it's a necessary one. Teaching values and proper behavior starts the first time your little one does something that's just not right.

Here are some tips to keep those "ouches" to a minimum:

THE BITER

Try to determine if she is teething, hungry, tired, stressed, curious, needing attention, or just frustrated.

I had a mom call me to ask what to do about her eight-month-old biter. Each time she nursed, the baby bit her. The first time it caught her so off-guard she said "ouch" really loud and the baby laughed. Now it is a source of entertainment at mealtime...Yikes! While the first time might seem cute, try not to laugh.

If it has been hours since your little one had a snack, serve her something healthy.

If your toddler is overtired, turn on some soothing music and curl up on the sofa together for a quick power nap. Just be sure it's not too close to bedtime.

Don't try to have an intelligent conversation about biting when your toddler is in the throes of crying. Timing is everything.

If your toddler is teething, offer her something to soothe those aching gums. Cold things seem to feel the best: frozen bananas, juice pops, frozen bagels, or even ice water. And never underestimate the power of child's

Get some books about biting to read together. Two great books I recommend: *Teeth Are Not For Biting* by Elizabeth Verdick and Marieka Heinlen and *No Biting* by Karen Katz.

pain reliever. (Check with your pediatrician first.) Hatching those teeth can really hurt!

If your toddler wants a toy from another child and bites her, an immediate "no" is in order. Using the five-minute rule is really helpful. Set a kitchen timer for five minutes and let each child have a turn with the toy in question. Any longer can seem like an eternity and bring out even more frustration.

If your toddler manages to bite her friend before you can jump in, make a big deal over the other child. Giving your child all the attention, even negative, is rewarding her for an unacceptable behavior.

If you see your toddler bite another child, step in immediately and say, "Teeth are not for biting. Look at Jill crying. You hurt her. You need to say you're sorry."

Offer your toddler something that she *can* bite; an apple, a pear, or some carrots are good choices. *And never leave her unattended for a second while she is eating.*

If biting occurs when your toddler is frustrated, suggest a fun physical activity to release her frustration. A game of catch, beanbag toss, or a running race should do the trick.

Some biters do well by transitioning to a quiet activity such as looking at books or watching an age-appropriate video. Offer a time and place to be calm.

Don't overreact. If your toddler is biting to get your attention, she will be very aware of your first reactions. And it won't matter if it's negative attention.

If your toddler is a habitual biter, make a sticker chart. One sticker for each day she doesn't bite. Five consecutive stickers earn a small reward. Positive reinforcement works great for all of us.

Never bite your toddler back. This will only reinforce negative behavior. "If mommy bites, I can too!"

THE SCREAMER

One more shriek and you're going to lose it!

Make sure your toddler understands the difference between an inside voice and an outside voice. Screaming is not an inside voice.

Get down to your toddler's level, look her in the eyes, and whisper, "We do not scream when we want something. Please use your inside voice."

Let her know that you will not respond unless she stops screaming. Tell your toddler you can't understand what she wants when she is shrieking.

Pay attention to when the screaming stops and calmly listen to what she wants. This is perfect for teaching her cause and effect.

Use all your self-control to not give in to her demands no matter how many times she screams.

Walk out of the room. It's not fun to scream if you're all alone.

Try to keep *your* screaming down to a minimum even if a snake or

Here's a fun book to read about throwing: *Watch Me Throw the Ball!* by Mo Willems.

mouse frightens you. Hearing mommy scream only reinforces your toddler's fear and shows her it's okay to scream.

THE SPRINTER

These tips should help if your toddler thinks it's a riot to run away from you.

While it's really cute to see that little naked bottom running away while the bath water is getting cold, try not to reinforce this behavior. It's a tough one to break.

Be careful if your toddler doesn't understand the difference between a game and a request. "Quick, Mommy's going to catch you" is only fun when it's time appropriate. Not when you're going to be late for work or preschool.

My Mouth Is a Volcano by Julia Cook is a great read about anger and frustration.

Give your active toddler plenty of opportunities to burn off that excess energy. A stop at the park, a game of catch, or a speedy walk around the mall will help keep your little one from doing a disappearing act at the bank.

If you don't have time for some physical activities before running your errands, make sure and give your toddler something to do at each stop. Holding your purse, handing the slip to the dry cleaner, giving the money to the teller are a few things that work well.

Don't forget to praise your toddler for being a good helper. There's nothing better than positive reinforcement.

Always insist that your toddler hold your hand in a public place, the mall, the grocery store, etc. There is no letting go or you leave the premises.

THE BOSS

Many toddlers think they are in charge. They try to tell everyone what to do. And while a certain amount of bossiness is normal and an indication that your toddler is becoming more confident, it's just not appropriate behavior when you're only three-feet tall.

When my daughter was a toddler, her disappearing act scared the life out of me. I had just pulled the car into the garage during a fierce snowstorm. I got her out of the car first and told her to stand next to me while I got her baby brother out of his car seat. It took one second for her to disappear. I was yelling for her, crying, and got totally hysterical. Just as I was about to go call my husband and the police she came running out from behind our detached garage. I didn't know whether to spank her or hug her. The hug won out!

Toddlers don't realize they are not the center of the universe and will try anything to get attention. Don't ever tolerate rude behavior. When your toddler is trying to take control, firmly let her know that she's not in charge.

But let your toddler make some decisions on her own. If you're a control freak and make all the decisions, she'll only want to assert herself more. Give her two decisions a day. For instance, "Do you want to wear your red skirt or your blue one? Do you want toast or an English muffin for breakfast?" Small decisions will build up her self-confidence.

If you ever hear her say, "No, I'm the boss!" nip it in the bud. Immediately let her know she is not the boss. But be sure to use a firm tone without anger.

THE INTERRUPTER

Each time the phone rings or you are trying to carry on a conversation in person your toddler thinks it's time to ask you a million questions, hang on your leg, or say, "Mommy, mommy, mommy." While this is just another normal part of your toddler's development, it can be downright annoying.

When your toddler interrupts, make sure that she just wants attention and the house is not burning down or another emergency is about to arise.

Let your toddler know that when you are on the phone, she will have to wait until you are finished to talk to her.

If she insists on interrupting, set a kitchen timer for three to four minutes, letting her know that she will have her turn when it rings. Any longer is nearly impossible as patience is not a virtue when you're a toddler.

Try to keep your phone calls down to a minimum. A forty-five-minute talkfest with your best friend just won't work when you have an active, awake toddler. Save your gossip for girl's night out or after she goes to sleep.

If you must make business calls when your toddler is awake, plan a quiet activity for her before the call. Coloring, sticker pictures, painting with water are some good ones that don't need your assistance. As a last resort, pop in a video.

One mom told me she kept interrupting her toddler when she tried to tell her something. The toddler got so frustrated and said, "Mommy, let me talk."

If it's not a business call, let your caller know at the beginning of the call that you only have a few minutes because your toddler is awake.

Make a phone box. Place some age-appropriate toys in a special box that she can only play with when you are on the phone. New is fun and different. Just make sure they don't need mommy's help.

Let your toddler know ahead of time if you will be having a visitor. Set some ground rules and stick to them. Can she be a part of the visit? Does she have to go in the playroom? Toddlers and surprises are not a good fit.

If your toddler interrupts when you are having a conversation with someone in your home, redirect her. Ask her to make you a coloring picture. Or excuse yourself from your guest, and find a few toys that will keep her interest for more than two minutes. Puzzles are good as are crayons and paper.

And don't forget to praise your toddler for being such a "good girl" while mommy was visiting with Mrs. Prince.

THE THROWER

Toddlers do not understand the concept of cause and effect. When they throw it's fun! They don't think about mommy getting angry, the dog getting hit, or the mess it's going to make...they just throw. So unless you've played lots of ball or beanbag games, this is just another activity in the eyes of your toddler.

Show your toddler what she can throw and where. Tell her the ground rules and stick to them. "Ball throwing is only outside, but the beanbag game is okay in the playroom."

Teach your toddler how to collect and throw the laundry in the washer.

Teach her how to throw the trash bag into the barrel.

Once you set up the rules, try your best to be consistent. If you tell her no pillow throwing and then have a pillow fight, your toddler won't know what the rules are.

If your toddler tries testing the waters and throws an inappropriate object like wooden blocks or metal trucks or other non-throwable toys, remove it immediately and say, "These toys are not for throwing!"

If you have a toddler that thinks it's fun to throw food, immediate correction is in order and the meal is over. No second chances on this one. And don't worry about her being hungry. She would be eating and not throwing if she was starving.

THE ABCS OF TODDLER CARE

Children seldom misquote you.
They more often repeat word for word what you shouldn't have said.

—Mae Maloo

BEHAVIOR CHART

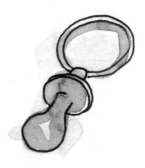

Using a behavior chart is a simple, step-by-step way to change challenging toddler behavior. The following page has a blank chart for you to fill out. Focus on only one behavior at a time. You don't want to overwhelm your toddler! For the top of each column, write a short description of the behavior that you would like to see. Buy a pack of small, star-shaped stickers and a pack of larger, gold star stickers. Add one small star to the chart to show that your toddler needs to work on a chosen behavior. Add another small star to mean better job and keep on working. A big gold star means good job!

Remember to be specific and positive when trying to change your child's behavior. Ask for a quiet voice or soft feet instead of "stop that!" Toddlers respond better to positive requests. In no time, your toddler will say, "I did it!"

BEHAVIOR									
	1	2	3	1	2	3	1	2	3
MONDAY									
TUESDAY									
WEDNESDAY									
THURSDAY									
FRIDAY									
SATURDAY									
SUNDAY									

TAKE YOUR FINGER
OUT OF YOUR NOSE!

Embarrassing Toddler Moments

Oh, look how cute, your little one found her nose. "Mommy is so proud of you. You're such a big girl!" Mistake number one, drawing attention to habits that are not always pleasing...nose picking, tush scratching, hands down the pants, humping inanimate objects, sticking things up the nose or in the ears, putting hands down mommy's blouse! I can feel my face turning red as I remember those days!

Toddlers have no inhibitions. When something moves them, they're not the least bit embarrassed. They don't ask for approval, they just go for it. And what could be so wrong with that? Learning about the world without all the social mores is the perfect way for your toddler to reach her milestones and to feel

Parker Picks by Deborah A. Levine is a great read for your little nose picker!

secure. But when these habits rear their ugly heads in public, yikes! Rest assured, this is all normal and just a part of self-discovery. However, as we all know, social etiquette is a must in our society. So it's our job as parents to set the limits and to teach our little ones acceptable behavior.

Remember, trial and error is the only way your little one will learn about the world. Yes, it will be embarrassing at times, and you may wonder why it's so tough to be a parent. But take a deep breath and when your little miracle does something that makes you want to run and hide, know you're doing the best job you can. And rest assured...this too shall pass.

Here are some tips to help make those learning moments a little less embarrassing:

When your toddler puts her finger in her nose, don't tell her how cute and smart she is. Gently remove it from her nose and go on with what you're doing.

Always carry a pack of tissues with you. When your toddler shows you the prize she just pulled out of her nose, whip that tissue out as fast as you can.

If your toddler proceeds to put that little booger in her mouth, after you say "Eww," a gentle but firm "Please put that in the tissue" should happen immediately.

Be prepared to correct your toddler more than once until she gets it. One sentence only, "Please take your finger out of your nose now or do you need a tissue?" says it clearly.

Hands in the pants, Oy! This is a tough one because it feels good. If you have a *young* (1–2 years old) toddler and he has just started using the potty, ask if he has to go potty. If the answer is no, lean down to his level and tell him to take his hands out of his pants and gently remove them. No explanations needed. He won't hear your words anyway. You will have to repeat this a number of times before he gets it.

If your toddler is *older* (3–4 years old) and it's not a potty issue but he just won't take those hands out of his pants, it's time to give a short age-appropriate explanation as well as tell him to go into his room if he won't stop. Remember, to a toddler, touching oneself below the belt is no different than touching his nose. If it feels good he'll do it.

One dad's story went like this: "I was in Home Depot with my wife and three-year-old toddler when he asked to go potty. As we walked out of the restroom, my adorable little son very loudly asked mommy, 'Why is daddy's pee pee bigger than mine?' Innocent but so embarrassing!"

If your precious is always scratching her little bottom, you may want to check for that dreaded schmear. If she's just started using the potty, she may not be an expert in the wiping department yet.

If your little girl thinks it feels good to rub against the corner of the sofa, a gentle correction is in order. Once you've stopped blushing, take her hand, tell her that's not okay, and redirect the behavior to a book, a toy, or to helping mommy. Just another normal toddler behavior to make mom or dad blush!

If you notice your toddler trying to put things up her nose or in her ears, immediate redirection needs to happen, as this can be dangerous. Firmly tell her not to stick things up her nose and give her a toy, some paper and crayons, or any activity that she enjoys. There have been many pediatrician visits to remove a Cheerio, pea, or other foreign object from a toddler's nose or ears. Distraction and redirection, the name of the toddlerhood game!

When your toddler makes an inappropriate remark out in public you have a few choices:

- You can ask her to apologize to the unsuspecting person.
- You can apologize for her.
- You can quickly leave the scene of the crime.

If she's old enough to understand, talk about what makes people different: blue eyes, green eyes, small or large feet, etc. But keep the conversation short, sweet, and to the point. To a toddler, who knows very little about etiquette and decorum and even less about what hurts people's feelings, remarking on a wide man's girth is as innocent as remarking on a "pretty flower" or a "big red truck." (H. Murkoff et al, p. 328)

If your little one has a meltdown in a public place, don't point to her and ask, "Does anyone know whose kid this is?" And try not to bribe her to stop by offering candy or a toy. You're only rewarding bad behavior. Gently pick up your precious and give her a hug. She wants your attention and hugs usually work great. If she's not too out-of-control, you can also try to redirect this behavior by giving her a task that will help mommy. If there's a pattern to her meltdowns, try to schedule those errands for a better time. If you don't have the luxury of working around your toddler's schedule, bring her a healthy snack containing protein. Cookies or fruit are not the best choices, as a sugar rush will only make things worse. Tantrums happen when your toddler needs some type of attention, food, a nap or she just doesn't feel good.

When your toddler does something inappropriate, don't give her a lecture and tell her she's a bad girl. After the first four words, she will only tune you out. Tackling each behavior as it happens, keeping words to a minimum, and being a good role model is the key to parenting a toddler.

Remember, it doesn't take much to distract a toddler and redirect them. Bringing along a small book or toy when you go out in public is great preparation for those embarrassing moments.

Be sure that all your child's caregivers are on the same page when it comes to inappropriate behavior. Discuss the consequences when these behaviors rear their ugly, embarrassing heads.

THE ABCS OF TODDLER CARE

Children are unpredictable.
You never know what inconsistency they're going to catch you in next.
—*Franklin P. Jones*

Don't worry that your children never listen to you;
worry that they are always watching you.
—*Robert Fulghum*

MR. SANDMAN,
BRING ME SOME DREAMS!

Toddlers and Bedtime

Your toddler has had a full day. She went to preschool in the morning and then the two of you took a special trip to the zoo. She played in her make-believe kitchen while you made dinner, had a bath, read a story, cuddled, and now lights out...not! Are you serious, you are ready to fall on your face and your little precious is wide-awake asking for water, one more story, and another kiss! Where is all this energy coming from?

Each toddler is different and you may have drawn the straw for the one that isn't going to go to sleep without a fight. And you thought getting up every three hours with her as a baby was tough. Here are some reasons why toddlers have a difficult time settling down for the night:

Number One: There is a lack of routine and each night bedtime
is different.

Number Two: She is overtired.

Number Three: She had a late nap.

Number Four: She thinks she's missing something.

AVERAGE SLEEP NEEDS OF TODDLERS (FROM THE *THE MOTHER OF ALL TODDLER BOOKS* BY ANN DOUGLAS)			
Age	**Daytime Hours**	**Nighttime Hours**	**Total Sleep Hours**
1 year	2–2.5	11.5	14
1.5 years	2	11.5	13.5
2 years	1.25	11.75	13
3 years	1	11	12

HERE ARE SOME TIPS TO HELP WITH THOSE BEDTIME BATTLES. WHERE TO START:

Set up a routine that will work each night and stick to it no matter who is caring for your toddler. If bedtime is 7 pm, keep it that way. Consistency is the key to easy bedtimes. Straying from the routine can be very confusing to your toddler.

Figure out your toddler's sleepy cues when deciding on a bedtime. Eye rubbing, hair twirling, or lying on the floor are just a few signs that it's time for bed.

If you are a working parent, don't let the guilt of not seeing your little one all day get to you. And letting her stay up late so you feel better is not a good idea.

Let your toddler make some choices during the bedtime routine, such as which pj's to wear or picking out an outfit to wear the next day are simple enough but keeps her involved. And it's great for self-esteem.

Make sure your toddler's activities are low-key before bedtime. Now is not the time to do Disney sing-alongs. Reading a book and cuddling on the sofa works great!

It's Time to Sleep, My Love, by Eric Metaxas and Nancy Tillman, will have your little one's eyes closing before you know it.

Let your toddler know bedtime is coming soon. Advance notice will allow her time to wind down. Saying, "It's time to get ready for bed, please put your toys away now" gives her the direction she needs and will make your life easier.

Set a kitchen timer if your toddler has a difficult time listening and transitioning. When the bell rings, it's bedtime.

Many parents find a warm bath helps their little one relax. But others find it too stimulating for their toddler. Remember, there is no rule that says bath time has to be right before bed. Every child is different and you make the rules.

If you offer a bedtime snack, be sure it contains a protein and a carbohydrate. The carbohydrate will make her sleepy and the protein will keep her full. Cheese and crackers or yogurt are good choices. Chocolate, cookies, soft candy, or ice cream are not.

Carbohydrate-rich foods containing the natural sleep-inducing chemical tryptophan, may help your toddler relax and calm down before going to bed, explains Elizabeth Pantley, author of *The No-Cry Sleep Solution for Toddlers and Preschoolers*. Avoid sugary, processed carbohydrates such as a bowl of sugary cereal or sweet toddler cookies. Three to five whole grain crackers with a tablespoon of hummus, a scrambled egg, a lightly toasted piece of whole wheat bread served plain or with a light coating of peanut butter (as long as he doesn't have a nut allergy), or tofu yogurt are healthy, calming snacks.

Keep bedtime snack portions small even if your toddler didn't eat a good dinner. Offering a meal before bed is not wise for her digestive system.

If your toddler skipped her nap, try your best to stick to the daily bedtime schedule. Don't let her take a catnap before dinner or put her to bed early. It could disrupt her sleep pattern for the entire week.

Many toddlers won't sleep without their pacifier, bottle, or you. Try to break these habits sooner than later as you may find your little one calling out for these crutches at the end of each sleep cycle.

If your toddler doesn't like to sleep in the dark, purchase a night-light that delivers soft light.

Toddlers are perfectly capable of getting themselves to sleep. Do not get into the habit of rocking her, lying in bed with her, or any other habit that will be impossible to break. A kiss, a hug, a "goodnight" and then make your exit.

Your toddler does not need to eat in the middle of the night. Don't let her coerce you into a midnight snack. Breakfast will be here soon enough.

If your toddler gets thirsty, a sippy cup filled with a very small amount of water is okay. Don't fill it up or you may be changing sheets in the middle of the night.

Many toddlers may talk, cry out, or make noises when they sleep. Try your best not to panic and go running into her room at the first peep.

For information on nightmares and night terrors, read my chapter titled "'Mommy, There's a Monster in My Closet.' Toddler Fears."

TODDLERS AND CRIBS

If your toddler is still sleeping in a crib, do not allow her to have large toys, pillows, or stuffed animals in there. It's very tempting to try to use them as a step to climb out of the crib.

Make sure the crib is not near any blinds with cords, mounted pictures, or any other items with ties or strings that could end up around her neck. **Safety always comes first.**

Crib bumpers make great steps for toddlers who want to be out in the other room with mommy. If you haven't already taken them out, now is the time.

If you are thinking about purchasing a crib tent to keep your toddler from climbing out of her crib, before your purchase, make sure to check out the company and their product reviews. Many crib tents have been recalled. For more information, www.babyin-structions.com has an up-to-date Recall page.

If your toddler has figured out how to climb out of her crib, it's time to transition to a bed.

When my daughter was sixteen months old, I put her in the crib for a nap and went downstairs. All of the sudden I heard a big bang coming from her room. I ran up the steps as fast as I could, thinking she fell out of the crib. As I went into her room I hit her in the head with the door as she was trying to come out. She had figured out how to climb out of her crib! Talk about mother guilt!

FROM CRIB TO BED

Talk to your toddler about sleeping in a "big girl bed." Make a big deal but don't overdo it.

Two of my favorite books about moving from crib to bed are *Big Enough for a Bed* by Apple Jordan and *My Own Big Bed* by Anna Grossnickle.

When talking to your toddler about moving into a bed, use her stuffed animals to demonstrate. Go through the entire routine from tucking them in, turning on the night-light, kissing goodnight to closing the door. This may sound silly, but it will not only better prepare your toddler, it also will help allay any fears she might have.

Set a regular bedtime routine and make sure it's working before transitioning your toddler to a bed.

If you are going to move your toddler to a bed before a new sibling arrives, give her four months for the transition.

If your toddler will be staying in the same room as the baby, putting the bed in the same place as the crib was will make things easier.

If you are going to be moving into a new house, try to move your toddler into a bed before the move. It's tough enough to have to adjust to a new room.

Don't move your toddler to a bed if you are working on potty training. One thing at a time is the key to success.

Before the big event, let your toddler help pick out the new sheets and comforter. Being a part of each step will make the transition easier.

If your toddler has a favorite blanket or lovey, make sure it goes on the new bed.

Picking out a new stuffed animal to sleep in the "big girl bed" with her can also be very comforting.

If you used a white noise machine in the nursery, continue to use it.

Many toddlers have an easier time falling asleep to music. Choose an instrumental lullaby CD that is soft and comforting. Turn it on before you tuck her in and make this a part of the bedtime routine.

Many parents transition their toddlers by starting them on a mattress on the floor. There is no right or wrong, it's your choice.

If you will be transitioning her to a bed with a mattress and box spring, whether it is a twin, queen, or king, make sure to buy bed rails to prevent your toddler from falling out. It will take her a few weeks to get used to the space. It's much different than a crib.

If you are going to continue to use the monitor, don't show your toddler where the camera is located. One mom told me that her toddler would not stop waving and making faces when she was supposed to be sleeping.

When the big night arrives, start the routine an hour earlier. And don't forget to tell her what a big girl she is and how proud of her you are.

If your toddler keeps calling out to you once you put her to bed, a firm

"Goodnight, mommy will see you in the morning" is imperative. Running into her each time she calls is a bad habit to start.

A parent educator and PBS Ready To Learn consultant says: "One of my best hints to get children to sleep is read to them for twenty minutes and then say, 'Let's count all the people who love you.'"

If your toddler just can't fall asleep those first few nights, set a kitchen timer for ten minutes and sit with her until she is comfortable and starts to drift off to sleep. Gradually decrease the time you

spend with her at bedtime until she can do it on her own.

Don't bribe your toddler with gifts or special surprises to get her to sleep in her bed, as this is a tough one to stop. Just remember that this is all new and will take some getting used to.

Patience is a virtue. This transition is another wonderful milestone in the life of your toddler.

THE ABCS OF TODDLER CARE

People who say they sleep like a baby usually don't have one.
—Leo J. Burke

"MOMMY, THERE'S A MONSTER IN MY CLOSET."

Toddler Fears

One minute your toddler is happily playing with her toys and the next she is shrieking in fear as she sees a lion in a commercial on the television screen. "Mommy, will the lion come get me?" How can your easygoing toddler turn into such a nervous Nellie? She's too young to have worries and, besides, mothers are supposed to worry, not toddlers. Toddlers want to be independent and are constantly testing the waters. But sometimes those waters have waves too big to jump. Think about the book *The Three Little Pigs* when the big bad wolf "huffs and puffs and blows the house down." Adults know that it's make-believe, but many times a toddler has a difficult time figuring out what's real and what's imaginary. The world can be a scary place and while toddler anxiety can be a little disconcerting, realize it's normal, expected, and part of her emotional and cognitive development. She will outgrow these fears with some patience and understanding from you.

Here are some pointers to help deal with those scary moments:

SEPARATION ANXIETY

This happens around six months of age and may rear its ugly head again in toddlerhood. There's no quick fix but consistency is the key.

Dr. Ari Brown says, "Separation anxiety peaks around fifteen to eighteen months of age—that's probably not the best time to experiment by leaving your child for the first time with a new babysitter!"

Leave your toddler with someone that she knows and trusts. If it's going to be someone or someplace new, make the introduction a day or two before the event.

Acknowledge your toddler's feelings: "I know you feel sad when mommy leaves you."

Let your toddler know you will be leaving but will always come back.

When staying at a place other than her own home, allow her to bring a favorite lovey or toy.

If you are leaving your toddler at home with a sitter, show the sitter your child's favorite lovey or comfort place in your home as some tears may come.

Give your toddler a kiss inside each hand to hold while mommy is away. It's like having mommy with her.

Never sneak out. It's not only disheartening and frightening to your toddler but breaks the trust between the two of you.

Always say good-bye, making it short and sweet. Long and drawn-out good-byes only make separation more difficult.

Carry some special stickers with you and before you leave put one on her shirt for being such a big girl.

If you are upset, don't let your toddler see it; only smiles and happy faces during good-byes.

If your toddler won't let go of your leg or the tears won't stop, ask the caregiver or babysitter to redirect your toddler to a fun activity.

FEAR OF NEW FOODS

Many toddlers will turn up their noses at new foods. They don't like the way they smell, look, or feel. But part of growing up is being exposed to many different foods. It's your job to introduce her to healthy, delicious foods that make mealtime a celebration.

Here are some suggestions when she says, "Yuck, I'm not eating that!" Remember your toddler doesn't know new and different can taste good.

When it's time to eat, sit down together and make it a family occasion.

Offer a variety of healthy choices. And make the plate look appetizing.

Use a small plate with toddler-sized portions. (No paper plates, please.)

Let your toddler help you prepare meals when introducing new foods.

If she's reluctant to try a food, you take a bite and say "Yum!" Be a good role model.

Tell your toddler you have the "one bite" rule. She needs to take at least one bite to taste the food. If she doesn't like it after the one bite she doesn't have to eat it. And don't waver on this one.

You can also try reverse psychology. Tell your toddler she's not allowed to eat it. You might be surprised what a challenge will do.

If your toddler flat-out refuses, move on. Mealtime should not be a battleground.

Never force your toddler to eat. You want mealtime to be happy, not a setup for a future eating disorder.

Here's a great book to read to a picky eater: *Eat Your Dinner, Becky Sue*, by Kimberly Bennet.

Continue to offer new foods at various intervals. They may look better in another week.

We all have individual tastes. If your little one has done the "one bite" rule and just doesn't like something, forget it. There are plenty of healthy alternatives.

FEAR OF THE DARK

As I write about this fear I can still feel the shivers when my mother turned off the light at night. Toddlers have a vivid imagination that can be governed by the books they read, the videos they see, and their playtime with their friends. While this is healthy and means your toddler is on track, it can also present some real challenges when the lights go out.

Talk with your toddler about her fears and be positive and honest. While these fears may seem silly to you, they are real to her. Ask her what scares her and let her talk about them. Never say, "Big girls aren't afraid of the dark."

Be reassuring but don't go overboard. Keep things in perspective.

Before choosing a book for your toddler, read it first. If there are monsters (even friendly ones), fighting, or any type of aggressive behavior in the story, choose another one. Toddlers have vivid imaginations and sometimes have a difficult time distinguishing between real and make-believe.

When your toddler comes home from a playdate, preschool, or grandma's, ask if they read any books or watched any videos. Things that may be off-limits in one home may not be in others. Be prepared.

If your toddler is afraid of the dark, try playing a game with her. Ask her to close her eyes and think about something fun she likes to do like going to the park or getting ice cream. Positive association while being in the dark can really help.

If your toddler wants her closet doors shut and her door open at bedtime, just do it. Pick your battles. But be sure to tell her if you will be closing her door when you go to bed or in the morning if that's your rule.

Make some "Monster Begone Solution" by filling a spray bottle with water and when those monster dreams appear in the middle of the night, spray them away.

Make a "No Monsters Allowed" sign that she has colored to hang on her door. It will keep those monsters out.

Take your toddler to the store and let her pick out a night-light that emits soft light. Being a part of the process makes her feel more in control. And it's easier to see that there are no monsters in her room if there's a little light.

Make a sticker chart. Give her a sticker for each night she doesn't get out of bed. When she earns five stickers in a row, a special treat is in order along with lots of hugs and kisses. Keep the treat small, a mini-celebration with make-your-own sundaes, or a trip to the pet store to visit the dogs; something that will let your toddler feel the victory but not expect a marching band each time she succeeds.

One mom told me that her toddler put his teddy bear by the door to stand guard and protect him from monsters while he slept.

NIGHTMARES OR NIGHT TERRORS?

The difference between Nightmares and Night Terrors (*Toddler 411*, A. Brown)

	NIGHT TERRORS	NIGHTMARES
Age	Older than 18 months	3–6 years old
Sleep State	non-REM	REM
Sleep period	First third of the night	Last half of the night
Consolable?	No	Yes
Easily returns to sleep?	Yes	No
Recall of the event?	No	Yes

Nightmares or dreams occur during REM sleep in the second half of the night. Your toddler will wake up crying and anxious but is consolable and may actually remember her nightmare the next day.

Night terrors occur during the first third to the first half of the night during the non-REM sleep. (A. Brown, p. 165) Toddlers will wake up screaming in terror, may sit up in bed, with eyes open and will look like they are totally awake and aware. But they are not. They are inconsolable and may not even recognize mommy and daddy. Night terrors usually happen the same time each night and can be caused by being overtired or stressed and most toddlers don't remember them. Here are some solutions to help when those night terrors strike: (A. Brown, p. 165)

Try to relax and understand this is perfectly normal behavior for many toddlers.

Don't turn on the lights. Go in to your toddler and make sure she is safe and can't get hurt or fall out of bed. Sit with her until the night terror passes.

Don't try to wake her up, you will only startle her more and the calming process will be tough and take longer.

Don't pick her up and bring her into your bed. This is another move that will startle her.

If night terrors happen the same time each night, Dr. Ari Brown says, "Set your alarm clock and wake your child fifteen to thirty minutes before his usual night terror happens. This will cause her to have a partial wakening, bypass the end of the cycle when the night terror occurs and move on to the next sleep cycle."

If the night terrors occur pretty regularly, a visit to the pediatrician may be in order.

Fear of Sudden or Loud Noises—Many toddlers are easily startled by loud or sudden noises like the vacuum cleaner, coffee grinder, food processor or even the agitation of the washer. There is nothing to worry about and be assured that she will outgrow this fear. Each toddler is different and her hearing may be more fine-tuned than others...totally biological.

When your toddler jumps you may jump too, but try to stay calm.

Don't swoop in and wildly say, "What's wrong?" Instead, say, "That was really loud. I bet it surprised you!"

Don't make a big deal with this fear. Say the above and let it go. Your toddler can and will sense your anxiety.

If you know your toddler is sensitive to a particular noise, give her some warning before it happens: "Get ready to cover your ears, time to grind the coffee for breakfast!"

Fear of New People—Many toddlers have no qualms about running up to a stranger and telling her about her toys. Others hang onto mommy's apron strings, stand behind her and won't come out. Both children are perfectly normal but as the parent it's your job to respect your little one's personality.

Don't ever force your toddler to hug, kiss, or shake hands if she's not comfortable.

Don't ever say, "What's wrong with you? You love Aunt Ruth." Shaming hurts and is embarrassing.

If you know your little one is cautious, give the other adult a quiet heads-up.

It's okay to let your toddler sit on your lap while you talk until she feels comfortable enough to venture on her own.

Don't let grandma or any other family members shame your toddler if she doesn't immediately warm up to them.

If you are in a playgroup situation and your toddler only wants mommy, sit on the floor with her until she's ready to play with the other children.

If you will be having a get-together and lots of new people will be coming to your house, prepare your child. Talk about how much fun it will be and who will be attending.

Ask your toddler to draw some pretty pictures to decorate the table for the get-together.

If you were shy and your toddler is old enough to understand, tell her about you when you were a little girl.

Fear of Water—Okay, so your toddler's not a fish. She likes to stay on dry land. The first mention of the pool, ocean, or even bath time can bring on those tears in seconds. Water fears are natural for many toddlers and may be evolutionarily programmed. But keeping your little one safe around water is priority number-one even if she's not going to be the next Olympic swimmer.

Don't ever pressure your toddler to go into the water.

Never, Ever make your toddler stay in the pool if she is scared. Not only is this dangerous but it is also a water fear setup for life.

Expose her to water when possible. Just taking her to the beach or pool regularly will help ease the fear even if she just sits and watches.

When your toddler starts to show interest, let her do it at her own pace. One day just the feet, next week maybe the entire body.

If her fear is not too great, sign her up for swimming lessons. But make sure to interview the teacher

One of my favorite tips to help a toddler get used to having water on her head and on her face is to buy some swimming goggles and let her wear them in the shower or bath. It's not only fun but also a good way to keep the water out of her eyes and to let her see it's not that scary!

first and not just do it because all the other moms take their toddlers to this class. You want an experienced, patient, and understanding teacher that has dealt with toddlers having water fears.

If and when your toddler decides that water is really fun, *never leave her unattended for a second.* Accidents happen in the blink of an eye.

Fear of Animals—Many toddlers are fearless when it comes to animals. They will run up to any dog (not a good idea), try to pet a cat, or run after a rabbit without a second thought. But others run the opposite direction as fast as they can when something furry appears.

If your toddler isn't afraid, teach her never to run up to a stranger's dog and put her hand, face, or any other part of her body near the dog. Always ask the owner if the dog is friendly and then gently show your toddler how to hold out her hand for the dog to sniff.

Teach your toddler not to go near your dog or anyone else's while they are eating. A big "No, No." Many children have been bitten during a pet's mealtime.

Teach your toddler to respect all animals. Rabbits, squirrels, and birds live outside and don't want to be held, touched, or chased.

If your little one is terrified of dogs, don't ever force her to pet a dog. It's scary for both of them and you never know what the dog will do when he senses fear.

If you are walking and your little one refuses to move because a dog is coming, suggest that you hold hands and pay no attention to the dog as you walk past, or cross the street if she is shaking with fear.

You can also pick her up until the dog passes. Forcing a toddler to do something that terrifies her may create a lifelong fear, which is never a good idea.

Talk about her fear when she's in a place that feels safe, like her room or yours. Not when the animal is close by.

Go to the library and check out some books about animals to read together. Or watch an age-appropriate animal video. *Ice Age* or *Madagascar* don't count, they're not real.

If you have a pet store that lets you play with the puppies, make a few visits as a special treat and let your toddler just watch.

When she is ready to pet and hold a puppy, show her how to do it.

But tell her that puppies can be wiggly and sometimes playfully bite little hands. Be ready to help.

Do not buy a dog because you think it will help your toddler's fears. It's not fair to either one of them.

Fear of Trying New Activities (climbing, jumping, going down the slide)—Just because you're a toddler and trying to assert your independence doesn't mean you're not afraid. Even though toddlers may see their friends going down the big sliding board at preschool and riding tricycles really fast doesn't mean they want to do it too. And that's okay. Toddlers mature at their own rate and that should be respected. Climbing Mt. Everest is not in the toddler rulebook!

The first rule of thumb when trying any new activity is to be sure your toddler is going to be safe, for instance, a helmet for bike riding, a sliding board and playground that is age-appropriate.

Don't ever force your toddler to try something when she is afraid. That's when accidents happen.

Don't tell her she's acting like a baby or compare her to her big brother or a friend. It's not only unconstructive but also downright mean!

Don't let another parent into the mix by offering to help your toddler go down the big slide just like her daughter. Politely tell the mom that you appreciate her help but you've got it handled.

Ask your toddler if she wants *you* to go down the slide with her, swing on the rope, etc.

If your toddler starts to try a new activity and changes her mind (climbs back down the sliding board steps), don't draw attention to it. Either ignore it and engage her in another activity or let her know you're so proud of her for trying and maybe next time she'll go down the slide.

Inasmuch as you want to, don't shout, "You can do it!" when she is gingerly climbing up the steps to the jungle gym. Just watch with pride.

Once she conquers an activity fear, let her know you understood. "I know you weren't sure you could go down the slide, but you did it! You should be so proud of yourself. Mommy is proud of you too!"

THE ABCS OF TODDLER CARE

Being a mother is learning about the strengths you didn't know you had and dealing with the fears you didn't know existed.
—Linda Wooten

BREAKING UP WITH YOUR BINKY

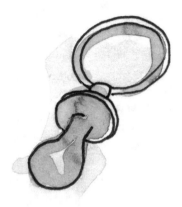

There is nothing more heart wrenching than hearing your toddler cry that first night she doesn't have her binky. When you first introduced it you never thought it would be her best friend, and soothe your little wonder at naptime, sleep time, and cranky time. And save your sanity when trying to stop your toddler's tantrum. As she grew from babyhood into toddlerhood, you would have never imagined she would hide her binkys in her underwear drawer, her play purse, and even her shoes so mommy or daddy wouldn't find them. Talk about attachment...Yikes.

So the big day has arrived, your toddler is two years old, ready to start preschool, and it's time to say "Bye Bye Binky!" Here are some ways to

"Kids who use a pacifier past age two are at risk for developing secondary bad habits—such as tongue thrusting and lip sucking—that can affect the growth of the mouth and teeth, making future orthodontic care more complex," says pediatrician Ari Brown, MD, author of *Baby 411*.

I know one mom who packed up all the binkys and took her three-year-old to the zoo to give the binkys to the animals. (She didn't really throw them over the fence but gave them to the zookeeper.)

make this transition a little easier.

Remember, you're the parent. You decide when it's time to take away the binky. Be consistent and no turning back once you make the decision.

Pack up all the binkys and let your toddler give them to a friend for her new baby.

Tie the binky to the string of a balloon and let it float into outer space. But make sure to remove the rest of the binkys in the house if there is more than one.

While you will have a few bouts of crying or whining, go cold turkey. And remember to use positive instead of negative reinforcement. The right way: "Mommy is so proud that you don't need the binky. You're such a big girl!" The wrong way: "Only babies have

One of my favorite books about binkys is *Little Bunny's Pacifier Plan* by Maribeth Boelts.

binkys. Stop acting like a baby!"

Make the binky taste bad. Ask your pharmacist for something safe to put on the binky. Many parents have tried THUM LIQUID™. Cruel but usually works after a few sucks.

Some parents have been successful by damaging the binky, by cutting off the top or poking holes in it. I am *strongly against* this method as it's not safe. Small pieces could come off and be a choking hazard.

Tell your toddler she can take all her binkys to the pediatrician's office to give to the newborn babies. But remember to call ahead so the nurse or office manager can come out, collect them, and say "Thank you."

Bring in the "Binky Fairy." Tell your child that she needs to give all her binkys to the Fairy so she can give them to all the new little babies. And sweeten the pot by telling her "binky fairies" leave surprises in return. Make a package containing all the binkys and leave it outside before bedtime. (Don't forget to remove it before morning.) Buy your toddler a token (a book is great), wrap it in pretty paper, and leave it on the table for your toddler to find at breakfast!

Lose her binkys never to be found. While there may be some tears, if it's lost, it's lost! After searching the house, choose a fun activity to do together. Baking cookies, coloring, or going for a walk are just a few suggestions.

Patricia Hamaguchi, a speech-language pathologist from Cupertino, California, and author of *Childhood, Speech, Language, and Listening Problems: What Every Parent Should Know*, says, "Even without noticeable problems, talking around a pacifier may limit your child's opportunities to talk, distort his speech, and cause his tongue to unnaturally flatten at rest." In some cases, with frequent use, it may also cause a forward protrusion of the tongue, which sets the stage for dental problems and the development of a "lisp" when producing the *s* and *z* sounds. For these reasons, Hamaguchi recommends eliminating pacifier use by about eighteen months.

Not all parents think binkys are a big deal and let nature take its course. One mom said once her toddler went to preschool and saw that the other children didn't have binkys, she didn't want hers anymore. Another mom told me her little one was so tired after a fun day at preschool she didn't need it to soothe her to sleep.

There's a great Sesame Street video to share with your toddler about Elmo giving up his binky. (http://bit.ly/M4bav6)

THE ABCS OF TODDLER CARE

If you haven't time to respond to a tug at your pants leg,
your schedule is too crowded.
—Robert Brault

IT'S MY POTTY
AND I'LL TRY IF I WANT TO!

Toddlers and Potty Training

You have three months before your toddler starts preschool and you're worried. She's not potty trained and there doesn't seem to be any hope on the horizon. You feel like you've tried everything from picking out the perfect potty with Dora on the seat to M&M bribery and nothing seems to work. Those big girl panties spend more time in the washer than on your "big girl"…Yikes. If she's still in diapers you won't be able to go back to work and that spells disaster in this economy. You need Plan B…maybe a preschool that accepts toddlers in diapers, a grandma who wants to babysit, or a change in work hours. Let's face it, you stand on your head, give out candy galore, and beg your little one to "just try for mommy!" But if your toddler's plumbing and mind don't connect, she's just not ready and there's nothing you can do that will speed up achieving this milestone.

SOME SIGNS THAT SHE IS READY

If you notice your little one stopping mid-play and squatting, grunting, or putting her hands in her crotch area, it might be a good time to start potty training. Your toddler needs to recognize those physical sensations that tell her bathroom time is now.

Other signs include:

- If she comes to you and asks to have a clean diaper.
- If she can stay dry for a few hours.
- If she knows what the potty is for.
- If she is able to pull her own pants up and down.
- If she wants to sit on the potty.
- If she tells you when she has to go on the potty.

THE EQUIPMENT

There are pros and cons when deciding whether to use the big toilet or a little potty. The decision is yours. There's no right or wrong.

Sometimes there is a fear factor when having to use the big toilet. It's high, she needs to climb up, and her feet can't touch the floor.

If your toddler is going to use the big toilet, purchase a small stool that

One mom told me that she planned on sending her three-year-old to day camp but he wasn't potty trained. She tried everything to potty train him but he just wasn't interested. After much looking, she found a day camp that would take her son if he was still wearing diapers. As she was getting little David ready for his first day of camp, she said, "David, let me put your diaper on." And he replied, "I'm not wearing a diaper to camp. I want to wear underwear. Big boys don't wear diapers!" And he never wore a diaper again...stubborn toddler!

is sturdy, made of wood, and not too high. Many of the plastic stools are too lightweight and can easily topple over.

One of the advantages of using the big toilet is not having to drag a little potty with you when going out of the house. And most businesses will let your toddler use their restroom if you ask nicely.

If the choice is to use a small potty, you can purchase an inexpensive, lightweight folding potty seat that fits on top of the big toilet. I love the Dora folding potty seat. ($12.96 online, $16.00 in stores.)

Put together a potty bag for the car: the folding potty seat, toilet paper, wipes, disposable plastic bags, and a change of clothes (just in case).

Teach your toddler not to touch everything in a public restroom. There is a great product called gLovies (www.gLovies.com), which will protect your children's hands from all those nasty germs. It's the perfect solution.

Weigh your time and options when choosing training pants. There are pros and cons to each one. As one mom told me, "While disposable training pants (or pull-ups) are convenient and can be great when going out, they are super-absorbent and very much like a diaper." Her toddler had a difficult time figuring out if she wet her pants. This type of training pants can falsely make a toddler think she is dry when she is really wet.

Jessica from Alabama said she was in Sears shopping for a new washer when her three-year-old wandered away. As she looked across the aisle he had his pants down, was sitting on the store's display potty, and said, "Look mommy, I'm using the big boy potty!" Jessica said she never ran out of a store so fast in her life!

Cloth training pants or underwear feel like "big girl" pants. The biggest drawback is containing accidents. You will always have to be on "puddle control" until she's totally potty trained. And your washer and dryer may be working overtime for a few weeks. Choose what works best for you and your family, as there is no right or wrong.

If you are going to be using cloth training pants, let your little one pick out the ones she likes best. It's all part of the process.

IT'S POTTY TIME

Talk about potty training with your toddler before you start the process and make sure she understands.

A study conducted at the University of Pennsylvania found that 4 percent of children are trained by age two, 22 percent by age two-and-a-half, 60 percent by age three, 88 percent by age three-and-a half, and 98 percent by age four. And while 70 percent of girls are trained by age three, just 50 percent of boys can make the same claim. The average age that children show an interest in toilet training is 24 months for girls and 26 months for boys. (A. Douglas, p. 249)

Go to the library to get a few books about potty training and read them with your toddler.

If she's ready to start potty training, relax. Your little one can sense your anxiety. Cool, calm, and rational is the name of the game.

Don't try to start potty training during a time of stress, new baby, vacations, or moving into a new house. Pick a time when things are nice and calm.

Summer is a great time to start potty training if your toddler is ready. Clothing is lighter and easier to pull down. I know one mom who dressed her toddler in a bathing suit during potty training. That was genius!

Pick a time when you will be home and not running around when you start potty training. Weekends work best for many parents.

Make sure everyone in the family is on the same page before you start potty training. There is nothing more confusing than inconsistency.

Everyone Poops by Taro Gomi is one of my favorites!

Don't be shy about using the appropriate words. No baby terms allowed here. A vagina is called a vagina and that's the truth.

Give your toddler the opportunity to view the same sex parent using the potty. It's much more effective than using a doll or stuffed animal.

When you take her into the bathroom, make sure she doesn't take all her clothes off. Many toddlers think potty time and birthday suits go hand in hand because many times she will have to use the potty before a bath.

If you have a boy, start him out by sitting on the potty backwards. It's easier to aim. And remind him that he has to point his penis down.

Most boys don't have the coordination to stand, aim, and pee until about thirty to thirty-six months.

Once he has mastered the sitting down technique, graduate to standing up. But let him know what the rules are: "Pee only in the potty." Potted plants, pets, and anything else are off-limits. You can purchase a product online called "Tinkle Targets" to help your little boy with his aim.

Teach your little girl to keep her legs together straight over the lip of the potty to keep from spraying urine.

If she is wearing a dress, show her how to tuck the hem of the dress into the neckline so it doesn't end up in the potty.

Make sure to teach your little girl to wipe from the front to back to avoid introducing bacteria into the vaginal area.

When wiping after a bowel movement, having your little ones use baby wipes instead of toilet paper is a good idea until they are pros at wiping.

Insist that your toddler wash her hands each and every time after using the potty. Setting up good hygiene habits from the start is a must.

If your toddler has an accident during potty training, don't get angry and scold her. It's called "training" for a reason.

Praise your toddler each time she is successful but don't go overboard. Using the potty is a part of life and shouldn't feel like an award-winning performance.

If you need an incentive, make it manageable: one piece of candy, a sticker chart, or whatever works best. Buying big expensive toys or videos are just not necessary. A small token for success is enough.

If you're not comfortable using an incentive because it feels like bribery, don't use it. There is no right or wrong. Every child and family has different needs.

One mom shared that during potty training, she loaned her toddler a favorite baby doll for an hour each time she pooped on the potty. After the hour it went back to mommy until the next time. What a great incentive and a reward that worked for her.

Sometimes peer pressure is the key. If your little one is already in preschool, seeing the older children use the potty may be enough to spark her interest.

Keep your pets out of the bathroom while potty training. Not only are they a distraction but it's not their time or place.

As tough as it is, try your best not to compare your child's progress to others. Each child trains on her own schedule.

Many pediatricians recommend *American Academy of Pediatrics Guide to Toilet Training* by Mark Wolraich.

If you're spending more time washing underwear and begging your little one to "please try," she may not be ready. Put it on hold for a while and try again when she seems more interested. Potty training should be a learning experience and not a struggle.

THE ABCS OF TODDLER CARE

One day you're a superstar because you "pooped" in the toilet like a big boy, and the next day you're in the principal's office because you said the word "poopy."

—*Dav Pilkey,* **Captain Underpants and the Preposterous Plight of the Purple Potty People**

Rewards are great when potty training your toddler. Fill a jar with bright red cinnamon candies or M&M's. I gave one candy for peeing on the potty and two for pooping and lots of "Woo hoo's, good job!"

—*Jill M., Texas*

When potty training your little boy, float some Cheerios in the potty for a straight aim. What a fun way to learn.

—*Suzanne, Maine*

MY POTTY TRAINING CHART

ACTIVITY	MON	TUES	WED	THURS	FRI	SAT	SUN
Walked over to potty							
Pulled down pants							
Sat on potty							
Made pee in potty							
Made BM in potty							
Cleaned up after going potty							
Pulled pants up							
Washed hands							

"TAKE THAT BABY BACK!"

Preparing Your Toddler for a New Sibling

Your belly is starting to grow, the morning sickness has passed, and you're wondering how and when to tell your "first baby" that she will soon be a "big sister." What is the right time and the best way to make this transition easy?

You've asked your friends with two children a million questions. Their answers made you feel a little less apprehensive. Randi has one little girl and swears that reading *There's a House Inside My Mummy*, by Giles Andreae, every night made little Sydney feel important. Andrea's mother Karen said, "Visiting friends with new babies made her feel like the best big sister in the world!"

While you know that welcoming a new sibling into your family is a time filled with joy, your first baby has no idea of the changes that are about to occur. She's been the center of your universe for three years. It doesn't matter if your first child is a toddler or in second grade, preparation and positive reinforcement are the key words here.

The first few months are usually the most difficult. Transition takes time. But with the right tools, many naps for everyone, if possible, and lots of planning and patience, this second amazing event will be as good as the first.

Here are some tips to make the transition a little easier for the "queen of the house":

Nine months can seem like an eternity to your toddler if you start the discussions the minute the little blue line appears on the test. Try to wait until the second trimester, when your tummy starts expanding.

Let your toddler's age and comfort level govern your discussions. It's not necessary to share graphic details with a two-year-old.

Don't over-talk the part about the baby crying. This can unnecessarily raise your toddler's anxiety level.

If you have friends with infants, try to visit them when their baby is awake. Your little one will see that sometimes babies cry and that's okay.

Attend a sibling preparation class together at your hospital or library.

Don't take your toddler to your doctor visits. Watching mommy get a pelvic exam is pretty scary.

If you're anxious about the baby's arrival, share your feelings with your

One of my friends took her three-year-old daughter to a doctor's appointment with her. After the appointment, Bethany came out and loudly proclaimed, "Mommy has a circus in her gina!" Talk about mommy having a red face!

husband or friends. Never burden your toddler with these adult fears.

Plan a special time for you and your toddler to look through her unused baby toys and pick out a few for the new baby. As you choose, talk about when she was a baby. This is great for your toddler's self-esteem and her role as "big sister."

Start a new ritual with your toddler *before* the baby arrives. Something as simple as cuddling with her for ten minutes before bed each night is perfect—just the two of you sharing your love.

If it's time to move your toddler into a "big-girl bed," make the move at least four months before the baby is born. You want to leave enough time for this new adjustment. There is nothing worse than having two sobbing children in the middle of the night.

If your toddler will be going to a new preschool or day care when the baby arrives, leave plenty of time for this change—one to two months, if possible. Too many changes all at once will only make the situation more difficult for the entire family.

If your little one is already in preschool, prepare the caregivers in advance so they may talk about the big event.

Ask your toddler's preschool teacher to do something special when the new baby arrives. Reading a book about big sisters could be just the ticket. I love *Best-Ever Big Sister* by Karen Katz.

Take a picture of the new baby and her big sister. Give it to your toddler to take to her preschool for show-and-tell.

William Sears, MD, suggests, "replaying your child's babyhood."

One mom told me her toddler gave the new baby one of Lo Lo the dog's toys and said, "This is not our baby, it's Lo Lo's baby!" Another mom said that when the baby was two months old, her three-year-old told her it was time to take the baby back. That she spent enough time visiting!

Sit and page through her baby picture album showing her what she looked like coming home from the hospital.

If you are planning a home delivery, introduce your child to the midwife or doula a few times before the event.

Having your child witness the delivery is a personal decision. But remember, it can be terrifying to hear or see mommy hurting and not comprehending that this will result in a wonderful miracle.

Let your child know where she will stay and who will be with her while you are in the hospital and try a few dry runs in advance. This is not the time to spring a new babysitter on her.

Take the new "big sister" to the store to pick out a special gift *for* the new baby.

Make sure to give "big sister" a special gift *from* the new baby as well.

Don't be upset if your toddler reverts back to babyhood, wanting a bottle or diaper. This is normal. She is used to being mommy's center of the universe 24/7 and wants that attention back.

Plan a special activity with your toddler once or twice a week while the baby is napping. Make cookies, color together, or watch a special video like *Three Bears and A New Baby* by Sesame Street or *Arthur's Baby* by Marc Brown.

If you live near relatives, ask them to come over and do something special with your toddler or take her for an outing. Alone time without that baby will do wonders during this transition.

When the baby is awake, encourage your toddler to help. Ask her to get you a burp cloth, hold the bottle, or pick out an outfit for the baby to wear. It's so important for her not to feel left out.

Show your toddler how to be gentle with the baby. Remember, this is all new for her. Please be patient if she doesn't do it right. Guide her hands until she understands. But never leave your toddler alone holding the baby. Accidents can happen in the blink of an eye.

Your toddler may get aggressive and try to hit or pinch the baby. Relax, this is normal behavior but one that *will not* be tolerated. Focus on the behavior and not her. Firmly tell her, "Hitting the baby hurts." Don't say, "You're a bad girl for hitting your new baby sister."

If your toddler continues to hit or pinch the baby, take her into another room immediately where a time-out is in order.

Make sure your baby is always securely strapped into the swing or bouncy seat even if she looks too tiny to fall out. One bump by your toddler could spell disaster. Keeping your children safe is always your number one priority.

Kodak moments are great, but remember to take pictures of both your children. There is nothing more disappointing to a toddler than looking at the new pictures and she can't find any of herself.

BOOKS FOR TODDLERS

Baby on the Way, William Sears, MD, Martha Sears, RN, and Christie Watts Kelly

The New Baby, Fred Rogers

Spot's Baby Sister, Eric Hill

THE ABCS OF TODDLER CARE

Making the decision to have a child is momentous. It is to decide forever to
have your heart go walking around outside your body.

—*Elizabeth Stone*

A parent's love is whole no matter how many times divided.

—*Robert Brault*

STARTING PRESCHOOL
FOR THE VERY FIRST TIME

Can you believe it? Your toddler is ready to start school and *your* stomach is in knots. She has been carrying around her backpack, loaded to the top for weeks and can't wait, but you can. Don't be so hard on yourself. You checked out lots of preschools, talked to the directors and teachers, looked at the rooms, the toys, the playgrounds, smelled the smells, went through the checklist, and chose the perfect one. Now the big day is almost here.

Yes, this is the first time your "baby" will be spending her days without you. While it's exciting, you wonder how anyone can do as good a job as you? Relax…take a deep breath and pat yourself on the back for being such a great parent! Your little one wouldn't be ready for preschool without all your tender loving care.

The following tips should make this transition easier for everyone.

GETTING READY

Visit your toddler's classroom with her and meet the teachers a few times before the first day.

Borrow some books about preschool from the library and read them together.

If preschool starts earlier than little Jody is used to getting up, try to change the schedule a few weeks before school starts. There is nothing more frustrating than trying to get a tired, cranky toddler out the door during the morning rush.

What to Expect at Preschool by Heidi Murkoff and Laura Rader is fun to read.

Make sure your toddler knows how to wash and dry her hands as well as how to use the right amount of soap. Hand washing happens many times throughout the day in preschool.

If she has just finished successful potty training, make sure she knows how to wipe herself properly and completely.

If there are certain supplies you will need to purchase before school starts, let your toddler help. Picking out a new lunchbox and backpack will make her feel like such a "big girl."

Take your toddler with you when you drop off any supplies before school starts. The more she visits the school, the easier the transition will be.

If your toddler will be napping on a mat at preschool, be sure to ask her teacher if she can bring a special lovey, blanket, and mat cover to keep in school for naptime. Having things from home always feels better.

Make sure all your paperwork is filled out and filed with the school before the first day. If your toddler has any type of allergies, make sure to tell her teacher as well as adding it to the paperwork in red. Many preschools are now "nut-free" as many toddlers have nut allergies.

Make sure the teacher posts your child's name and allergies on a board or cabinet in the classroom in clear view. There's bound to be a substitute teacher in there at some point.

Ask your toddler to pick out her clothes the night before, giving her two outfit choices. She will feel like such a big girl when she's part of the process.

A few days before the first day of preschool, begin packing your child's lunch and let her eat it from the lunchbox at the kitchen table. Demonstrate how to take the food out of the containers, pack what's reusable back into the box, and throw out (or recycle) what isn't. (H. Murkoff et al, p. 824)

If you need to pack a lunch, do it the night before and let your toddler help choose what she wants to put in her lunchbox.

Don't worry if your toddler wants the same thing for lunch each day.

As long as it's healthy and she eats, variety may not be her spice of life at this age.

Do a dry run a few days before school starts with everything from picking out her clothes the night before, packing lunch, eating breakfast, and getting dressed and ready. Then go to the park and have a fun morning! You can never start a new routine too early!

THE BIG DAY

Get yourself ready first before waking your toddler. You never know what unforeseen things may arise.

Wake up your toddler a half hour earlier that first week. Getting ready may take longer than you think.

Don't worry if she doesn't want to eat her usual breakfast that first week. Change isn't always easy. Don't try to force her to eat. She won't starve.

While it's great to make a big deal of the first day of school, don't go overboard. It will just make your little one nervous.

Don't invite all the relatives over for the big morning. No one needs the extra hoopla.

Try to treat this special day like a new but normal day even if you have butterflies in *your* stomach. Toddlers are really good with nonverbal communication so make this a positive experience in spite of your nervousness.

Keep your fears to yourself and show your toddler the happy and positive side, no negativity. Preschool is fun and she will pick up on your frightened vibes and be scared too.

Mommy tears are normal. Let them flow *after* you've dropped off your toddler. There is nothing more frightening than seeing mommy cry.

The first day of school is usually rougher on mommy and daddy. If possible, ask your husband or partner to come along and plan a special celebration breakfast for the two of you after dropping off your little one. This is a big step for all of you.

If there are centers set up in the classroom, let *your toddler* pick the one that looks best to her. Becoming independent and making choices is so important during the toddler years.

If your toddler is having a shy morning, walk her over to a new friend and stand with them until they start playing.

If you are going to take pictures, make those Kodak moments short and sweet. The longer you stay, the more difficult it is to leave.

Before you leave, get down to your toddler's level and tell her that it's her job to have fun at school and your job to go to work.

If your little one wants to know when you will be back, ask the teacher what activity the class will be doing at pick-up time and share it with your child. "Mommy will be back after story time." Association is easier than watching the hands on the clock.

When it's time for you to leave, plant a special kiss in each of your toddler's hands to hold for safekeeping until you return.

Never sneak out. Let your toddler know you are leaving and will *always come back.*

When it's time for you to leave and your little one just won't let go of your leg, as her crying gets louder and more dramatic, ask the teacher for help. Then use all your willpower to walk out the door. Your toddler will be fine and the teacher should know what to do.

If this is an everyday occurrence, ask the teacher if your toddler can bring a special lovey with her each morning. And let your toddler know that it goes in her cubby when school starts.

One good-bye is enough. No matter how tempting, don't come back for more. Your apprehension will only upset your toddler.

If *you* are really nervous, ask the teacher to call you midmorning the first week with a short progress report. And keep the call short. Most teachers are more than happy to accommodate so *you* feel better.

If someone else will be picking up your toddler, make sure to let the office, teacher, and your toddler know before your good-bye at the drop-off. Make sure this person is on your pick-up list and include her phone number and contact information.

Ask the teacher to call you if your little one doesn't settle down. But remember, those first few days are a transition for everyone and the teacher should be able to handle it. This too shall pass.

Ask for a classroom roster and plan a "get acquainted" meeting with the other parents.

If you feel uneasy about *anything* in the school or classroom, *don't keep it to yourself.* Ask questions immediately. Never go to work with that nervous lump in your throat. And remember, no question is a silly question.

Starting preschool is a wonderful new chapter in all your lives. If you can walk out of the classroom each day with a smile on your face and warmth in your heart, then you know you've made the right decision. This is one milestone to be proud of.

THE ABCS OF TODDLER CARE

While we try to teach our children all about life, our children teach us what life is all about.
—*Angela Schwindt*

PRESCHOOL CHECKLIST

Finding the perfect preschool for your toddler can be very scary. How can you possibly trust another person with your precious bundle? You want a preschool where the toddler care is the best, the school is the cleanest, and the teachers are experienced, warm, and fuzzy. And you want to make sure there are lots of stimulating activities as well as age-appropriate toys, puzzles, and books to help your toddler reach her milestones.

Does this really exist? Hmm…And how will you know when you've found that perfect place? A place that feels totally comfortable when you drop off your toddler each morning. A school that will provide your toddler with the love, nurturing, and care she needs and be the perfect substitute when you can't be with her.

The following checklist should help make your decision a little easier. Print it out and take it with you. And don't be afraid to ask *any* question. Nothing should be off-limits when it concerns your toddler.

PRESCHOOL INTERVIEW CHECKLIST

When you call for an appointment, does the director speak to you or connect you to an assistant? Yes ❏ No ❏

What is the director's policy for having you visit the school?

_____

_____

Does the director keep you waiting more than a few minutes when you arrive? Yes ❏ No ❏

Does the director give you all the time you need to talk about the program and answer all your questions satisfactorily? Yes ❏ No ❏

Does the director show you the school's Mission Statement? Yes ❏ No ❏ If no, why not?

_____

_____

_____

Does she give you a booklet containing information about the school? Yes ❏ No ❏

Is she willing to supply you with references? Yes ❏ No ❏

At first glance, does the preschool look clean? Yes ❏ No ❏

Does it smell clean? Yes ❏ No ❏

Is the preschool licensed by the state? Yes ❏ No ❏
Is the license posted? Yes ❏ No ❏ If no, why not?

_____

_____

_____

Does the school do a background check before hiring a teacher?
    Yes ❏ No ❏
What kind of experience do the teachers have?

_____

_____

_____

THE TODDLER ROOM

Is the toddler room clean? Yes ❏ No ❏
Are the electrical outlets covered? Yes ❏ No ❏
Do the cabinets have childproof locks on them? Yes ❏ No ❏
Do you see any cleaning spray bottles sitting on the counters?
    Yes ❏ No ❏
Why aren't the cleaning supplies locked up, as it's a Health Department
    Rule?

_____

_____

_____

Do you see anything that would be dangerous lying around? Yes ❏ No ❏

Is there a locked medicine box in a safe place? Yes ❏ No ❏

Are the counters clean and uncluttered? Yes ❏ No ❏

Are the diaper-changing tables clean? Yes ❏ No ❏

Are there gloves available for diaper changing? Yes ❏ No ❏

Are there two sinks in the toddler room? One for the teachers and one
   toddler-height sink? Yes ❏ No ❏

Do the restrooms have toddler-sized potties and sinks? Yes ❏ No ❏

Are there soap dispensers and paper towels in the restrooms? Yes ❏ No ❏

Is there a nap mat for each toddler? Yes ❏ No ❏

Are the nap mats in good condition? Yes ❏ No ❏

Is the equipment in good condition? Yes ❏ No ❏

Are the toys, puzzles, and equipment age-appropriate? Yes ❏ No ❏

Are the toys and equipment cleaned with bleach water each day?
   Yes ❏ No ❏

Is there a bin to put dirty toys that get used during the day?
   Yes ❏ No ❏(For dropped toys, or toys that other toddlers chew on)

Is there happy music playing in the room and lullabies if it is naptime?
   Yes ❏ No ❏

Is there a library corner with age-appropriate books? Yes ❏ No ❏

Is there a dress-up corner for make-believe? Yes ❏ No ❏

Is there a play kitchen area with lots of fun supplies? Yes ❏ No ❏

Is there a pitcher filled with water and paper cups available all day?
   Yes ❏ No ❏

Is there a fire exit door with a sign posted above it? Yes ❏ No ❏

Does the room look like a place your toddler could have fun, explore, and blossom? Yes ❑ No ❑

Do you have an overall good feeling about the room? Yes ❑ No ❑

STAFF

Are there two teachers for every fifteen toddlers? Yes ❑ No ❑

Do the same teachers take care of the toddlers each day? Yes ❑ No ❑

Do different teachers come in for the late shift (3–6pm)? Yes ❑ No ❑

Is there a large teacher turnover and why? Yes ❑ No ❑

_____

_____

Do the teachers have CPR and First Aid Certification and is everything up-to-date? Yes ❑ No ❑

Do they know the Heimlich maneuver? Yes ❑ No ❑

Who has the authority to dispense medicine to a toddler?

_____

_____

Are the teachers friendly and eager to tell you about themselves and the program? Yes ❑ No ❑

Do the teachers act in a professional manner? Yes ❑ No ❑

Do the teachers look clean and neat and are they dressed appropriately? Yes ❑ No ❑

Are the teachers warm and responsive to your toddler when you visit? Yes ❑ No ❑

Do they tell you about the daily activities? Yes ❏ No ❏

Do they take the toddlers outside at least once each day (weather permitting)? Yes ❏ No ❏

Do they have circle time each day? Yes ❏ No ❏

Do they have specialists that come in for music, movement, etc.?
Yes ❏ No ❏

Do they send home daily reports? Yes ❏ No ❏

Do they want to know your toddler's schedule at home? Yes ❏ No ❏

What is their illness policy?

_____

_____

Are there conferences or just daily check-ins? Yes ❏ No ❏

Are you allowed to talk directly with the teacher by phone or just the director if you need to call? Yes ❏ No ❏

What are their rules for visiting your toddler at school?

_____

_____

What is the policy for drop-off and pick-up?

_____

_____

If someone else will be picking up your toddler do they need a special card, password, driver's license, or any other type of identification?
Yes ❏ No ❏

Does the school use the *same* substitutes all the time? Yes ❏ No ❏

Do you have an overall good feeling about the school, teachers, and toddler room? Yes ❏ No ❏

BLYTHE'S FINAL THOUGHTS

If you like the preschool, drop in unannounced.

Before you make a decision, call with any questions.

If you get the cold shoulder or you feel like they are too busy and you are unimportant…

FIND ANOTHER PRESCHOOL.

Once your toddler is enrolled, if you are told you can't visit anytime… FIND ANOTHER PRESCHOOL.

If the facility looks, smells, or feels dirty…FIND ANOTHER PRESCHOOL.

If the teachers are dressed inappropriately…FIND ANOTHER PRESCHOOL.

If the staff seems unhappy and not having fun…FIND ANOTHER PRESCHOOL.

Would you feel good leaving your toddler at this preschool each day?

Yes ❏ No ❏

If you feel great about the preschool then sign the papers. But if something feels amiss, even if you can't figure out what it is, go with your intuition—it's usually right!

Above all, you want to be able to enjoy watching your toddler blossom and grow in her new environment knowing you made the right decision.

IT'S PARTY TIME!

Fun and Affordable Toddler Birthday Parties

With preschool about to begin, your toddler's social calendar is filled with birthday parties each weekend. Her own birthday is just two months away. How can you compete with gymnastic bonanzas and fully catered events including professional entertainment?

In this day and age I wonder what parents are thinking when planning their children's birthday parties. They go so overboard that it's ridiculous. The true message of a birthday loses its meaning!

Many parents spend anywhere from three hundred to fifteen hundred dollars without so much as batting an eyelash! They hire limos to pick up the children, live bands for music, make goodie bags in excess of ten dollars, give Build-a-Bears for party favors, and serve champagne to the parents!

One family had a party for their five-year-old and fourteen of her closest friends at a very ritzy hotel serving high tea that cost thirty-five dollars per child. If that isn't crazy, I don't know what is.

This is not the message we want to send to our children. Feeling entitled is so wrong. And yes, money can make life easier, but it isn't a substitute for honesty, integrity, love, and caring about others. These are the lessons we want to teach our children from the beginning, not how to outdo their friends.

FOUR THINGS YOU DON'T WANT TO DO

Spend money without restraint and falsely send the message that your child is entitled to all of these things.

Try to out-party her friends. Kids are mean and will drop your child if her party was better than theirs and that really hurts.

Working parents sometimes try to compensate for their lack of time with expensive gifts. This too sends the wrong message.

Do not have a catered meal for the parents. And alcohol for the adults is a big "No No!" Whose birthday is this anyway?

Here are some tips to help you structure a meaningful and fun-filled birthday celebration:

Make sure your party is age-appropriate.

The rule of thumb is to invite one more guest than your child's age.

If your child goes to preschool, invite the entire class. You don't want to send a message that it's OK to hurt someone's feelings.

Or you can invite *one* best friend. Go to a movie or rent a video and make a special lunch and dessert together!

Plan an exercise party. Put a music or exercise video on and let each child take a turn leading the exercises. Serve cut up vegetables and fruit with several kinds of dip. What fun!

Plan a "book party." Instead of bringing a present, request that each child bring a book. Have them sit in a circle and ask each child to talk about the story. Make pretty cardboard bookmarks using craft supplies. Donate the books to a charity and let each child take their bookmark home. What a creative party favor!

Plan an arts and crafts party. Buy water bottles or sun visors at the dollar store. Put out glue, yarn, buttons, sequins, markers and let the toddlers decorate to their hearts' content. Use this as their special party favor.

Plan a video party. Choose an age-appropriate video (animated and humorous are good choices). Make popcorn, have an ice cream sundae bar, specially decorated birthday cookies, and water colored with fruit juice to drink. Spread a big blanket out on the floor and turn down the lights. What fun!

Make two cupcakes for each child and ask them to ice and decorate them. Save one for a party favor and put a candle on the other one so everyone can blow out the candles together. Then it's time to eat their creation! A great celebration with a lot less mess.

Ask each parent to bring a toy for a homeless child, food for a soup kitchen, or a can of dog food for the SPCA instead of a gift. What a wonderful way to teach children that not everyone is lucky enough to have all the creature comforts they have and how important it is to pay it forward. Have a circle time and talk about those less fortunate and then celebrate with cake and ice cream. This party covers everything!

Plan a family birthday celebration. There's no rule that says you have to invite the world. Family celebrations are sometimes the ones your toddler will remember the most! Plan a special birthday meal to cook together and surprise

One family had a party that met at a pet store on Adoption Day and brought a can of pet food to donate. Then they went to McDonalds for Happy Meals and ice cream. Giving back and having fun doesn't take much effort.

Here are a couple of my favorite birthday books to read together: *Curious George and the Birthday Surprise* by H. A. Rey, Margaret Rey, and Martha Weston and *Happy Birthday to You!* by Marianne Richmond.

your toddler with a cake. And remember to have the camera ready for some wonderful Kodak moments. It will make your hearts smile.

THE ABCS OF TODDLER CARE

All the world is birthday cake, so take a piece, but not too much.
—*George Harrison*

"MOMMY, I DID IT ALL BY MYSELF!"

Toddlers and Milestones

All of the sudden your toddler is doing lots of new things. She is walking, trying to talk, and wanting to feed herself with a fork and spoon and you are excited. But at the same time when you talk to your friends, their toddlers are not doing the same things. Your best friend's toddler talks in complete sentences and you can understand her. Your little sweetie is so cute but mispronounces many words and sometimes you can't understand her. Is there something wrong with her? Does she need speech therapy? Yikes…it's scary!

The first rule of thumb no matter how difficult is to try not to compare. Each child is unique and will reach their milestones when they are developmentally ready. It's truly not "one size fits all."

Try not to go on the Internet or buy tons of books. While they will provide interesting reading, the only thing you will end up with is confusion. Think of it this way, if you visit six Internet sites, you may get six different answers. And then what's right?

When watching your child as she blossoms and reaches her milestones, try to remember that nothing is etched in stone. There are age ranges as well as different stages that occur with each milestone, as you will see in the charts that follow. Just enjoy watching your toddler as she learns about herself and the world. And don't get crazy if she doesn't do things the same way as her friends. If she is healthy and happy, don't worry if she doesn't speak in complete sentences the minute she turns three!

However, if you really feel your toddler is lagging behind in one or more areas, don't hesitate to make an appointment with your pediatrician. You know your toddler better than anyone. But try your best not to jump to conclusions.

Here are the four basic developmental milestone categories:

Physical Milestones involve both large and fine motor skills. The large motor skills usually develop first, including sitting up, crawling, standing, and walking. The fine motor skills include holding a crayon, grasping a spoon, picking up small objects, and drawing shapes such as circles.

Cognitive Milestones are centered around thinking, learning, and solving problems. An infant learning to respond to a caregiver's singing and a toddler learning her phone number are examples of cognitive milestones.

Social and Emotional Milestones are centered on your toddler's understanding her emotions as well as those of others. Learning how to play with friends or in a playgroup are examples of social and emotional milestones.

Communication Milestones involve verbal and non-verbal language. These milestones include one-year-olds saying their first words along with toddlers developing a vocabulary to use when communicating with others.

The following checklist was developed by Denise Fields and Ari Brown, MD. You will see there is a range of ages for each milestone. They have determined that "normal" is at the level when 90 percent of kids have achieved each milestone.

GROSS MOTOR SKILLS	AGE ACHIEVED
Runs	13–20 months
Walks up steps with both feet	14–27 months
Kicks ball	16–24 months
Throws ball overhand	17 months–3 years
Jumps	22 months–2.5 years
Rides tricycle	3 years
Hops	3–4.25 years
Balances on each foot for five seconds	3.5–5.5 years
Skips	5 years

FINE MOTOR SKILLS	AGE ACHIEVED
Bangs objects together	7–12 months
Uses the thumb and forefinger to grasp objects (the pincer grasp)	9–14 months
Drinks from a cup	10–16.5 months
Puts a block in a cup	10–14 months
Scribbles	11–16 months
Uses spoon and fork correctly	13–20 months
Makes a four-block tower	16–24 months
Makes a six-block tower	19 months–2.5 years

Makes an eight-block tower	2–3.5 years
Has a hand preference	18 months–4 years
Can wiggle thumb	2.5–3.5 years
Can copy a circle drawing	3–4 years
Can copy a square drawing	4–5.5 years
Can draw a person with six body parts	4–5.5 years
Writes name	4–5 years

LANGUAGE AND COMMUNICATION SKILLS	AGE ACHIEVED
Follows simple directions	12–24 months
Follows instructions with two parts	18–24 months
Knows six body parts	18–24 months
Points to pictures when named	18–24 months
Understands in, on, and under	3 years
Recognizes some alphabet letters	3–4 years

EXPRESSION SKILLS	AGE ACHIEVED
50–200 word vocabulary	2–2.5 years
Speaks two word sentences	21 months–2 years
Speaks three to four word sentences	3 years
More than 500–1000 word vocabulary	3 years
Uses "I, you, we"	2–3 years
Can say name, age, and sex	3 years
Speaks four to five word sentences	3–4 years

SPEECH SKILLS	AGE ACHIEVED
Speech half understandable to strangers	17 months–3 years
Speech totally understandable to strangers	2–4.5 years
Normal dysfluency (stuttering)	3–4 years

SOCIAL AND INTELLECTUAL DEVELOPMENT	AGE ACHIEVED
Feeds a doll (symbolic play)	15–24 months
Brushes teeth with help	16 months–2.75 years
Washes and dries hands	19 months–3 years
Plays next to another child (parallel play)	2 years
Knows friends' names	2.25–3.25 years
Puts on a T-shirt	2.25–3.25 years
Recognizes and names one color	2.5–3.75 years
Plays board and card games	2.75–5 years
Brushes teeth without help	2.75–5 years
Understands taking turns	3 years
Gets dressed without help	3–4.5 years
Can tell which line is longer	3–5.5 years
Can recognize and name four colors	3–5 years
Plays with another child (associative play)	3–4 years
Counts five blocks	4–5.5 years
Counts to ten	5 years

THE ABCS OF TODDLER CARE

Parents need to fill a child's bucket of self-esteem so high that the rest of the world can't poke enough holes in it to drain it dry.

—Alvin Price

THERE'S A WHOLE LOT OF PLAYING GOING ON!

Toddlers and Playgroups

What could be better than playing with your friends when you're a toddler? But playgroups are not just for playing. They're also a time to learn about sharing, taking turns, and following instructions and rules. And for mom, it's a true sanity saver when you've been cooped up with your whining, bored toddler whose favorite word is "No!" It's also a great time for moms to visit, compare notes, and feel like they're not alone.

Remember, there is more than one type of playgroup. So do some research and choose the playgroup that will work best for you and your toddler. Careful planning is the key to success and fun. Let the happy chaos begin.

WHAT IS A PLAYGROUP?

The organized, paid group is one in which a set activity is planned, a teacher leads the playgroup, and there is a fee to attend. Parents are expected to participate while supervising their toddlers. The advantage with this type of group is not having to schedule or plan activities, nor host other children but you still get to meet new moms. If you miss a class, there are usually makeup classes to attend at a later date. Making new friends is always a plus in your life as well as your toddler's.

Mom-organized informal groups are free and rotate from house to house each week with one family hosting. The host is responsible for setting up weekly or biweekly playgroups and there is no charge. Each family takes turns hosting. Most of these groups are made up of friends that know each other and get along great. The hosting family is responsible for providing snacks and drinks as well as providing lots of fun activities and toys for the toddlers to play with. Toddlers look forward to playing with their friends while their moms meet to discuss the latest gossip of the week!

Organized playgroups are less formal and hosted by a synagogue, church, or other nonprofit organization. These playgroups may offer organized activities and outings, but sometimes it's just free play. There is no charge but you must sign up. The one negative aspect of this type of play-group is the adults falling victim to social politics, like breastfeeding versus bottle-feeding, co-sleeping, or other topics, which may cause disagreements among the attending moms. (Singer, p. 119)

THE PLAN FOR A SUCCESSFUL PLAYGROUP

Choose a time when you know your toddler and her friends won't be hungry or tired.

Short and sweet is the best plan. One to two hours should be perfect.

If you will be hosting, don't invite too many or too few children. You want it to be manageable and fun. With too many children you run the risk of someone getting hurt. And with too few, if

Some playgroups create a questionnaire for each parent to fill out including the name of parents and the toddler, home address, phone numbers, email addresses, allergies, and any other pertinent information they want to share. These go into a loose-leaf notebook that gets passed to the weekly host. See the end of this chapter for an example.

they get sick then no one shows up. Five to ten parents and children seems to work best.

Meeting once a week in the beginning is great for getting to know the other parents.

If your child has any special toys, put them away. Broken toys and meltdowns are not fun.

Put out a small number of carefully selected toys, games, and puzzles. Three toys per child are more than enough. Too many toys and games can create total chaos. And what a mess to clean up!

If you will be serving a snack, find out ahead of time if there are any food allergies and write them down.

FOR A MOM-ORGANIZED INFORMAL PLAYGROUP

At your first gathering, if you don't know each other, have nametags and markers available. Put your child's nametag on her back so she isn't tempted to pull it off. Once the toddlers are happily playing, ask each mom to share something about herself and her family.

Devise some rules and guidelines that you can all live with. Not every parent has the same philosophy.

Don't be afraid to talk about discipline and come up with some guide-lines as well.

Here are a few common questions that arise:

Do all moms have free rein with every toddler if a situation arises that needs some correcting?

Is it okay to put a toddler in time-out if needed?

How should you handle biting, pushing, hitting, or any other aggressive behavior? While discipline can be a touchy subject, knowing the rules at the beginning will prevent hard feelings between everyone.

What is the illness policy? Don't ever assume everyone is on the same

Some playgroups find it's easier to have each mom bring a snack for their own child.

page. A clear runny nose to one mom can create panic in another.

If the toddlers have younger siblings, is it okay to bring them to playgroup? Crying babies in strollers can sometimes be a real distraction.

Decide who will be responsible for providing the snacks at each playgroup.

If your playgroup is going to be two hours long, serving a snack at the halfway point provides a nice break as well as an energy boost for everyone.

If you will be providing the snack, choose something simple. Vegetables and dip, (toddlers love to dip), rice cakes and yogurt, cheese and crackers are healthy and easy to clean up.

Don't be disappointed if your toddlers play side by side and not together. Parallel play is normal for toddlers under three years of age and still lots of fun.

Offering arts and crafts that involve paint, glue, play dough, or any other type of art supplies is a recipe for disaster with a group of toddlers. Any activities that involve wet and sticky are better done at home.

Toddlers love freeze dance and musical chairs. They are easy concepts to understand at this age. Just prepare yourself for the excited squealing and laughter.

If it's summertime, water play is a great activity. Ask each parent to dress his or her toddler in a bathing suit and bring a towel. Supply them with squirt bottles, paintbrushes, cups, and even a baby pool if it's available. *Never* leave them unattended when there's water involved.

Having a dress-up corner can be so much fun! There are no limits to a child's imagination. Resale stores have lots of great outfits for reasonable prices.

If you're having a difficult time getting your toddler to do something during a playdate, be a good role model and show her how it's done. Penny Donnenfeld, Ph.D., says, "If your child is being rough with another child, guide her arms and show her how to hug that child."

Sharing is not a strong point at this age. A small kitchen timer is a must. Let each child set the timer for five minutes to play with that popular toy. When the bell rings, it's time to take turns.

If you must take away a toy, put it in a box labeled "Time-out Toys." You can remove the toy after ten minutes and try again.

When playgroup is coming to an end, set a kitchen timer and ask the children to clean up before the bell rings. Toddlers love challenges and making it a game is so much more fun.

When playgroup is over, don't hang around even if it's at your best friend's home. Teaching your little one that fun times come to an end is essential in life.

If you're not sure that this particular playgroup is for you, go to a couple of gatherings and give them a chance. Getting to know each other is part of the fun and sometimes snap judgments can be wrong.

A great resource when starting a playgroup is *The Playgroup Handbook: The complete, practical guide to organizing a home playgroup—with more than 200 activities for children 2 and up* by Laura Broad.

THE ABCS OF TODDLER CARE

No matter how calmly you try to referee, parenting will eventually produce bizarre behavior and I'm not talking about the kids.
—Bill Cosby

PLAYGROUP CHECKLIST

Here is an example of a playgroup checklist for an informal, mom-organized group.

Parents' Names _____

Child's Name_____

Address_____

Phone Number_____

Cell Phone_____

Dad's Phone Numbers _____

Siblings and Ages _____

Pediatrician's Number _____

Emergency Contact _____

Email Address _____

Allergies _____

Allergy Reaction _____

Allergy Treatment _____

Child's Likes and Dislikes _____

Are you available to host playgroup?_____

Any other information you would like to share? _____

"OH, THE PLACES WE'LL GO"

Traveling with Your Toddler

It's challenging enough to get ready to take a trip without our little ones. But planning for a family trip is one that could have you pulling out your hair in frustration. How do you know what to bring? Are you bringing too many clothes? Not enough? What happens if someone gets sick? So many questions and decisions. By the time you leave the house you are exhausted. But with careful planning your trip can be filled with fun, relaxation, wonderful memories, and lots of Kodak moments.

Here are some surefire tips to help keep stress to a minimum:

Before your trip, visit the dollar store and stock up on coloring books, paint with water books, and age-appropriate toys for your toddler. Give them to your toddler when she starts getting antsy. What could be better than something new! Make sure to dole them out one at a time, as you want to keep them coming the entire trip.

One mom told me when traveling with her toddler she takes noise reduction headphones for her toddler to use at sleep time. Listening to soft lullaby music helps her to fall asleep.

If your toddler doesn't sleep with a white noise machine, purchase one a few weeks before your trip. Turn it on each time your toddler sleeps. Most are small enough to fit in a carry-on. Take it on your trip to use for those bedtimes away from home. Not only will it feel more familiar but it also will drown out most of those outside noises.

If you have a small video player, stock up on age-appropriate movies and games for your toddler. Tablets like iPads work great for airplane or car travel. And you can rent movies at a nominal charge on iTunes.

Don't forget to bring along extra batteries, battery chargers, and photo cards.

Don't underestimate the power of music. Load up your iPod with child-friendly music. Toddlers love putting on headphones and bopping to their favorites when they need to sit still.

If you've just started potty training, wearing pull-ups with big girl panties on top is a good choice. There's enough to worry about during a trip without having to deal with potty accidents. Restrooms are not always accessible, especially during road trips.

Take along gLovies, which are disposable sanitary hand-covers, to use in those public restrooms and you won't have to worry about your toddler touching everything (www.gLovies.com).

Whether you will be traveling by car or plane, bring along lots of healthy snacks for your toddler. Buying them at convenience stores or at the airport can get very costly.

I was flying cross-country when I had the privilege of being seated in a row with a toddler and her mom. There was slight turbulence and the seatbelt sign was on. The three-year-old next to me had on her mom's big headphones. All of the sudden the entire plane heard "Hit Me with Your Best Shot" by Pat Benatar. This adorable toddler was belting out the song at the top of her lungs not realizing the rest of the plane could hear her!

Remember to bring some protein snacks for you as well. Nuts, protein bars, and fruit are great choices to keep up your energy.

If your toddler still uses a sippy cup, make sure to bring two. It will make your life easier if it falls on the floor. Sinks and water are not always close by.

Fill her sippy cups halfway with water. It is not only the healthiest but will dry quickly in case of a spill.

If your toddler is not a water drinker, make her juice with more water. Three parts water to one part all fruit juice.

Don't bring juice boxes. While they are easy to pack, one wrong squeeze and a change of clothes may be in order.

While it may be easier to offer your toddler caffeinated soda from the fountain when traveling, don't. Not only is the caffeine a bad idea if you want your little one to be able to sit still for more than two minutes, but the sugar is just not necessary.

Always take two changes of clothes, extra diapers, pull-ups, panties, wipes, and socks for your toddler. Spills can happen in the blink of an eye.

Bring a roll of plastic disposable bags for soiled clothing.

Remember to take a change of clothes for *yourself.* There is nothing worse than getting to your destination covered in sticky food.

Two of my favorite books to read before traveling on a plane are *Going on a Plane* by Anne Civardi and *My Plane Trip* by Cathy Beylon (a coloring book).

If you will be traveling on a plane, try to plan your trip for off-peak hours. It's tough enough to wheel through the airport with your toddler and all your stuff in tow without having to dodge those huge crowds.

For plane travel, purchase a seat for your toddler if possible. Sitting on mommy or daddy's lap for two or more hours is tough. And if there's turbulence, getting up is not an option.

If possible, reserve your seats when you book your tickets. And remember, car seats can only be installed in window seats on most airlines.

Make sure to arrive at the airport with plenty of time. Going through security with a toddler, stroller, and bags may take longer than you think.

Dress your toddler in easy, removable layers. You never know if the plane will be too hot or too cold.

Before the flight, do something active with your toddler. Take a long walk in the airport or run around if there is a space that is safe. Releasing extra energy before the flight will make sitting easier.

Give your toddler some water to drink during takeoff and landing to equalize the pressure in her ears. Be sure to fill up her sippy cup or purchase a bottle of water after getting through security before boarding the plane. Depending on a flight attendant to bring water is not a good idea. They get very busy and your request could easily be forgotten. If your toddler is not willing to drink, ask her to yawn. Those little ears can hurt.

If your toddler doesn't want to sit still during takeoff and landing, play the goldfish counting game with a paper cup for her and one for you. Put some goldfish in her cup and ask her to count them as she puts them in yours. Fifteen minutes of fun and learning instead of fifteen minutes of tantrums.

If you will be traveling on a wide-body or new plane, chances are they will have large fold-down changing tables in their restrooms. If not, ask the flight attendant if there are any empty seats in the back to use as a changing table. Make sure to dispose of your soiled diapers. Do not leave them in

If possible, bring along a replacement lovey just in case. You can never be sure you will find the exact one in another state.

the back of the seat in front of you. If there are no empty seats, you can struggle in the restroom or as a last resort, use your lap.

Always remember to bring first aid supplies, include cotton balls, tissues, antibiotic ointment, Band-Aids, and a package of M&M's for bravery. Boo-boos are a normal part of a toddler's life.

If you will be staying in a hotel, bring along plug covers, duct tape, and cleaning wipes. Cover the plugs, tape sharp corners, and wipe light switches, phones, and the remote control boxes. Making sure the room is clean and safe is so important.

Check for bedbugs. It's a sad fact of life but one that is prevalent in these times.

If you will be staying in a hotel, bring along your toddler's favorite lullaby CD that you play at home. Most hotels have CD players or you can request one. But call ahead to check. An iPod will work just as well. There is nothing more comforting than the sounds of home. And your toddler will be snoring away before you know it.

Remember to bring along your toddler's favorite lovey and bedtime book.

Try your best to stick to your bedtime rituals while away. Consistency makes everything easier. But don't stress if it doesn't happen.

If you will be hiring a babysitter when staying at a hotel, make sure she comes to meet you and your toddler a few hours before you will be going out. If you like the sitter and your gut feelings are good, keep your plans intact. Otherwise, forget about it. A night out is not worth the worry.

Here are some fun YouTube videos to watch about plane travel:
Airplanes taking off: http://bit.ly/PUH6c2
Airplanes landing: http://youtu.be/fmVEydDbh-c

THE ABCS OF TODDLER CARE

When preparing to travel, lay out all your clothes and all your money. Then take half the clothes and twice the money.
—Susan Heller

SURVIVING THE HOLIDAYS WITH YOUR TODDLER

The holidays are a time to celebrate and gather with family and friends. A time to enjoy the wonderful smells coming from the kitchen. To "ooh and ahh" over the new baby and blink in amazement when they see how much your toddler has grown. There is nothing better than enjoying each other, reminiscing, telling stories, laughing, sometimes crying but just sharing your love while creating memories to last a lifetime.

But when you have a very active toddler that has a mind of her own it's not always so easy. And while you are in charge, are you really asking too much of your toddler to sit still at a family dinner or to wear that adorable, scratchy dress and matching headband? The family would be crushed if your toddler couldn't be part of the celebration. Let's face it; there is nothing better than showing off your precious little miracle.

The following tips will help keep you and your squirmy toddler happy:

When planning, don't start talking about the holidays too far in advance. Two weeks can seem like an eternity to a toddler.

I love *Five Silly Turkeys* by Salina Yoon and *Counting Kisses* by Karen Katz (you know how relatives like to kiss little ones).

Visit the library and check out a few holiday books to read together.

If you'll be going to a religious service, before the celebration, show your toddler a picture of the seats and talk about what will happen during services.

If possible, plan a visit to the church or synagogue before the holidays.

Arrange a special meeting with the rabbi or pastor during your visit. Getting familiar with the surroundings before the holidays eliminates endless questions during services.

Visit the sanctuary and let your toddler stand on the pulpit or bema.

Play some holiday music at home and teach your toddler the words. What could be more fun!

If there are special wishes such as "Happy Thanksgiving" or "Merry

Christmas," teach them to your toddler so she may say it during the holidays. This is a great way to include her and wonderful positive reinforcement!

If you will be going to a synagogue during the High Holidays, talk to your toddler about the shofar and the funny sounds it makes. Youtube, under "shofar sounds," has great video demonstrations.

Talk about the special holiday foods and sample some before the holidays. Apples dipped in honey for Passover and Christmas Stollen make delicious snacks.

Plan a special time to bake together. Christmas cookies and challah are fun and easy.

THE HOLIDAYS HAVE ARRIVED

Select that special outfit the night before.

Ask your toddler to try it on and take a few pictures.

No matter how cute that trendy holiday outfit might be, make sure it's not too tight, hot, or itchy. Comfort is the operative word!

If grandma and grandpa live out of town and use Skype, call them and have your toddler model their beautiful holiday outfit.

HOLIDAY SERVICES

If you will be going to a religious service in the morning, wake your toddler an hour earlier than usual so there is plenty of time to eat breakfast and get dressed.

Let your toddler take a small picture book and lovey to services. Sitting for more than fifteen minutes with nothing to do can seem like a lifetime to a squirmy toddler. Having a quiet activity available really helps.

If your toddler wakes up out of sorts and is possibly coming down with a cold, do yourself a favor and let her stay home. Make sitter arrangements in advance just in case.

Firmly insist that your toddler eat a substantial breakfast. Growling tummies equal irritable toddlers.

Get yourself ready first and your toddler last. Toddlers sometimes take a little longer than expected. Leave enough wiggle room for the unexpected!

Make sure to have your toddler use the restroom before going into services.

Some services involve lots of standing. If your toddler doesn't want to participate, it's okay as long as she sits quietly.

Whispering is okay if she must tell you something important.

If your child is four or younger, bring along a healthy snack. A hungry toddler is a cranky toddler. But take her out of the sanctuary to enjoy her food.

If you know there is no way your toddler will last for the entire service, take turns with your husband so you each get to attend a portion of worshipping.

Have Plan B ready to go, whether it is lining up a sitter, taking shifts with hubby, or just staying home.

While it's wonderful to include your toddler in all the holiday activities, bringing her to a religious service may not be in the cards at this age. You want to be able to worship in a manner that honors your spirit without too many distractions.

THE FAMILY DINNER

If you will be having a holiday dinner in your home, let your toddler help you with the preparations.

Don't lose sight of the rituals. Not the holiday's rituals—your toddler's rituals. Keeping the daily routine as consistent as possible during the holidays will minimize the disruption for your toddler. (H. Murkoff et al, p. 778)

Ask her to color place cards for each guest, help set the table, or make special holiday cards for everyone. And tell her about each person that will be coming.

Remember, you don't have to be "Supermom." It's okay to ask your guests to bring a favorite dish for the holiday dinner.

If you insist on doing everything yourself, ask daddy to watch your little one while you prepare. Or better yet, hire a babysitter for a few hours. You may need daddy to set up the chairs or do "man's work" to help.

If you will be going to someone else's home and your toddler still takes naps, don't skip her nap to go earlier. Arriving a little late with a well-rested toddler could mean the difference between good and bad memories.

Give your toddler a snack before going to someone's house for holiday dinner. You never know what time the actual dinner will commence. And sometimes those adult hors d'oeuvres may not be on your toddler's list of favorite foods.

I had one mom tell me that she made special toddler-sized hors d'oeuvres and took them with her to grandma's house for cocktail hour.

Let your toddler pack a small bag of toys to take with her. Adults are just not that interesting when you're a toddler.

Go to the dollar store and stock up on some small toys. Take the surprise bag to the celebration and give it to your toddler when she just can't sit still anymore.

Pack a bag with your toddler's pajamas just in case the celebration runs later than you expected.

If your toddler won't let go of your leg and gets whiny, be patient. Being in a crowded room with lots of noisy and excited relatives takes a little getting used to.

When your eighty-year-old Aunt Rose wants your toddler to sit on her lap to cuddle and your toddler just isn't buying it, don't force her. Gently let Aunt Rose know that little Jessica loves her but is going through a shy stage.

If it's time to eat and your toddler isn't interested, forget about it. Pick your battles. She'll eat when she's hungry.

Arrange a signal with daddy ahead of time in case you need to make a quick exit. Leaving before your toddler's screams go over the top is not being rude. It's being considerate.

If it does get to be too much for your toddler, it's okay to say "thank you" and "good-bye." Listening to a toddler having a meltdown does not make for good memories.

Try to let go of the stress and enjoy the beauty of the holidays even if things don't go exactly as planned. Nothing is perfect and you can only do your best.

THE ABCS OF TODDLER CARE

Let us be grateful to people who make us happy; they are the charming gardeners who make our souls blossom!

—Marcel Proust

Families are like fudge, mostly sweet with a few nuts.

—Anonymous

WILL THIS RUNNY NOSE
EVER STOP?

As all parents know, the cold and flu season is just not fun. Will your toddler's nose ever stop running? And why can't she cover her mouth when she coughs? Her poor little lips are so chapped and her nose is so red. The two of you have been cooped up in the house for two weeks. The famous Rubber Ducky song, written by Jeff Moss, just keeps playing over and over in your head. You've read so many books you know the words by heart. She is bored and cranky and so are you. You've exhausted all the activities and games you can think of...now what?

Here are some fun activities that will make you both feel better!

Cynthia Boggs, an esthetician and mom, says avocado oil will soothe those chapped lips, red nose, and cheeks, plus, no chemicals, it's good for you. Take your little one in front of the mirror, saturate a cotton ball with avocado oil, and let her dab it on those sore red spots. Then see who can make the funniest faces...you will both be laughing in seconds!

Here is a great tip for chapped hands. Take two clean, white athletic socks, get out some markers, and let your toddler draw two eyes, a nose, mouth, ears, or whatever he chooses. You can also glue on some buttons, yarn, or any other objects. Pour a small amount of olive oil on your little one's hands, have her rub them together, and put the sock puppets over each hand for showtime! Another great tip from Cynthia Boggs.

Cynthia also says that if you happen to use indelible marker to make the above sock puppets, tea tree oil will remove the marker. It's nontoxic and won't hurt your little one or the environment.

Ask your toddler to pick out four red objects in the house. Pick three rooms to hide these objects in. Tell her to close her eyes, and hide them in a place she can reach. Then, set a kitchen timer for five minutes and tell her to look for the objects. If she can't find them, collect them and ask her to hide them from you. A great way to practice colors and numbers and so much fun!

If your toddler just wants to relax on the couch but is irritable and whining, play the number game. Ask her how many legs a cow has? Or how many wheels a car has? Variations: use pennies to count, M&M's, straws, anything that's easy to reach and safe. Take turns asking. Four-year-olds love this game and you don't even have to leave the couch!

Toddlers love stickers and they can be great entertainment for hours. Give your toddler a few pieces of construction paper and ask her to make special sticker pictures for the family. Stock up on stickers when you see a sale as you can never have too many! And this is one project that never gets old.

Making collages are lots of fun. Seat your toddler at a table covered with newspaper. Set out pieces of macaroni, yarn, ribbon, cotton balls, pipe cleaners, anything that you might have around the house that will stick to paper with glue and is safe. Give her a piece of construction paper, a glue stick, and let her make a masterpiece.

When she is finished with the collage, play the clean up game. Set the kitchen timer for two to three minutes, give her an empty garbage bag, and sing the clean up song while she makes her art area spotless. Sing: "Clean up, clean up, everybody everywhere. Clean up, clean up, everybody do their share!"

Most toddlers love to help clean and wipe anything. If your little one feels up to it, give her a clean cloth and ask her to make the table and chairs spotless. You can give her a spray bottle filled with a small amount of water if it won't be too messy. She can also wipe her toys.

Make a pretty necklace using yarn, Cheerios, buttons, and pasta with holes. First measure the yarn so it fits loosely around your toddler's neck. Make a knot in one end of the yarn and wrap a tiny piece of scotch tape around the other end so it's easy to thread through the objects. Then string away. There is nothing better than doing a project together!

Toddlers love to cook. If she isn't too congested and milk products are okay, making instant pudding is a favorite. Let your toddler do the pouring and mixing all by herself, with your supervision. What a great snack to share!

If her appetite isn't great but she likes scrambled eggs, crack the egg in a bowl, let her pour in a little milk and whip the mixture together while you do the cooking. Ask your little chef to make one for you too!

Cinnamon toast tastes really good when you are not feeling well. Let your toddler spread the butter and shake the cinnamon and sugar on top. Then, using cookie cutters, cut out fun shapes!

Instant oatmeal is another easy food your toddler can make by pouring, mixing, mommy heating it up, and then eating. The name of the game to getting better and feeling good is about doing it all by themselves!

If you just can't imagine reading another book to your little one, ask her to read it to you. And show her how to imitate the voices.

Here are some great books to read while your toddler is recovering:
Goldilocks and the Three Bears by Laura J. Bryant
Bear Feels Sick by Karma Wilson and Jane Chapman
Who's Sick Today? by Lynne Cherry

If your toddler isn't thrilled about taking a bath or shower when she doesn't feel well, give her pool goggles to wear in the water. It's fun and you know it will make her feel better.

So being cooped up in the house can be fun after all. The above activities should make your life just a little easier while the healing is happening. But remember, no matter what you choose, spending time together is how you create wonderful memories. And if you think back to your childhood, I'll bet you can all come up with a special memory that brings a warm, fuzzy feeling inside.

THE ABCS OF TODDLER CARE

Love is staying up all night with a sick child—or a healthy adult.
—David Frost

If you treat a sick child like an adult and a sick adult like a child, everything usually works out pretty well.
—Ruth Carlisle

MARY POPPINS, ARE YOU OUT THERE?

Finding the Perfect Nanny

You were lucky enough to be able to stay home with your precious the first year, but it's just not in the cards anymore. It's time for you to go back to work and you're nervous. After much discussion with your hubby, you've both decided that finding a nanny is the best solution. But how will you ever find a nanny that will love your toddler as much as you do? You know her little quirks, how she likes to touch her hair when she's tired, how to get her to eat vegetables, and how to calm her down when those tears start flowing. And who is going to teach her the alphabet, colors, and how to tie her shoes? Yikes...will you really be able to leave her with someone else?

THE FOLLOWING CHECKLIST WILL HELP FIND THE PERFECT SUBSTITUTE FOR YOU.

Name _____

Address _____

Phone Number_____

Cell Phone Number _____

Emergency Contact _____

Email Address _____

Agency _____ Phone Number _____

How long have you been a nanny?

Why do you want to be a nanny?

What do children like best about you?

What are your beliefs about childrearing?

What do you like least about being a nanny? Do you have any special pet peeves about parents/children/animals?

Do you have any formal early childhood development or childcare training?

Would you be willing to take classes to further your education in childcare?

How do you feel about having pets in the home?

Please provide me with your job history and performance.

Please supply me with four references including phone numbers and email addresses. (When you call them ask specifically what they liked or didn't like about this nanny.)

Please supply me with a copy of your CPR and First Aid certification and any other certificates you hold.

If not, would you be willing to take CPR classes and first-aid training?

Would you mind if I ran a background check on you?

Please supply me with your TB test documentation.

Describe your health history.

Do you have any personal responsibilities or health issues that could interfere with a regular work schedule?

Do you have children and would their care interfere with this job?

Describe your personality.

What are your dietary habits?

Do you smoke?

What hours are you available to work?

When would you be able to start working?

What are your salary needs?

If hiring a part-time nanny for an hourly fee, discuss schedule changes, days cancelled, and missing days. Does she expect to be paid if either one of you make changes?

Do you expect her to make up missed days?

Do you have future plans (school, job, marriage, etc.) that would put a
limit on how long you expect to be a nanny?

Do you have any trips planned when you will need time off?

Are you willing to do light chores while our child is sleeping? Which ones?

Would you ever be available to work evenings or weekends?

Are you available for overnights should the need arise? (For day nannies)

What kind of car do you drive?

Please supply me with your driver's license and insurance card.

Talk about properly putting the car seat or booster seat in the car.

Talk about taking your toddler in the car, where and when?

Discuss who pays for gas.

Would you bring your own food or expect meals to be provided?

Where does your family live?

Please provide me with a list of your emergency numbers (work, cell, and
pager).

How will you play and interact with my toddler (singing, dancing, going
outside, games)?

If my toddler were having a cranky day, how would you handle it?

What are your favorite activities to do with toddlers?

If my toddler won't eat, how would you handle it?

If you were bathing my toddler and the doorbell rings, what would you
do?

How do you handle temper tantrums?

How do you know when a toddler is sick and what would you do?

How do you discipline children? Can you share some examples?

How do you comfort children? How do you deal with separation anxiety?

What are some of the rules you've followed in other households that worked well?

Which rules haven't worked for you?

Would you be willing to follow my rules and disciplining/comforting strategies even if they're different from yours?

If I'm working in the house, will you be able to keep my child happily occupied without involving me?

Discuss the schedule and needs of your toddler.

Are you willing to take my toddler to the library and/or toddler classes?

Discuss the nutritional needs of your toddler and stress exactly which foods she may have and if there are any food allergies.

Discuss any medical issues that your toddler may have that need special care and make sure your nanny will be comfortable handling them.

Discuss any other household responsibilities (laundry, dishes, etc.).

Discuss the daily responsibilities the job will require.

Discuss childproofing the house. Does she understand what is safe and what is dangerous?

If you have a pool, what are the rules?

Do you know how to swim?

Do you know how to do life-saving techniques?

Talk about your rules of the house, including telephone use, having friends over, etc.

What is your gut telling you about this person? Will you feel comfortable leaving your toddler with her? If the answer is yes, check out her references, draw up the contract, and be confident that you've made the right choice.

THE ABCS OF TODDLER CARE

Sometimes the smallest things can take up the most room in your heart.
—Winnie the Pooh

IT'S TIME FOR DATE NIGHT

Choosing the Perfect Babysitter

It's Saturday night and you and your husband are dressed and ready to go out for the evening. The babysitter you hired was supposed to arrive fifteen minutes ago. You are pacing the floor and wondering whether you are just being nervous or your intuition says to cancel the night out. But one look at your husband and the guilt sets in. It's been months since the two of you have been out alone together. And you felt so good after interviewing the babysitter. She passed all your tests, but did she? Hmm!

Name _____

Address_____

Phone Number_____

Cell Phone Number _____

Emergency Contact _____

Email Address _____

Agency _____

Phone Number_____

INTERVIEW QUESTIONS

How many years have you been babysitting?

What ages of children have you cared for?

How old are you?

Have you completed a babysitting course? (For teenagers)

Have you taken a CPR and First Aid class that included the Heimlich maneuver and have you ever had to use them?

Do you drive or will you need transportation?

Do you have a curfew when you babysit?

Do you own a cell phone?

Do you smoke?

Do you mind taking care of our pet as well?

Do you have any allergies or medical conditions we should know about?

Do you know how to swim? (For families with pools)

How do you handle temper tantrums?

How would you handle my toddler if she won't listen to you?

What situation would warrant that you call us?

Can you supply us with three babysitting references?

BABYSITTER MUSTS

She arrives on time for the interview.

She is dressed appropriately with clean clothes, washed hair, and no funky body piercings.

She asks lots of questions about your toddler.

She shares her knowledge about toddler's likes, dislikes, and how she handles things.

She engages with your toddler during the interview and might even bring a book or toy to show her.

She is more than happy to share her references, experiences, and information about herself.

THE NEXT STEP

Discuss money before your babysitter arrives for the first job and make sure she understands.

Let her know if your food is off-limits and she needs to bring her own.

If your babysitter is a teenager, many times they will tell you to pay them whatever you want and then be upset when you hand over the money. If this is the case, tell your babysitter up front what you will be paying her per hour. And don't ask her if it's enough. You're the employer. No surprises, no hard feelings.

If your babysitter is going to be eating during the job, ask her to please clean up her dishes and the kitchen.

Let her know if she is allowed to cook.

Discuss the house rules. Is she allowed to have friends over, use the phone, etc.?

Tell her if you expect her to clean up your toddler's toys and play-room.

If she is going to be feeding or changing your toddler, write down detailed instructions and make sure she knows where everything is kept.

Let her know you expect to find the house in the same condition as you left it.

Hire her for a working interview while you are home but stay out of the way and let her take care of your toddler.

If your toddler is going through separation anxiety, tell her you will be home but the sitter will be playing with her while you do your work.

If you want to peek during the working interview, don't let your toddler see you. But you will know if she is having fun by the sounds you hear.

LAST STEP

When your babysitter arrives, show her where all your phones are located, how to use them, and tell her if you want her to answer your house phone.

Show her where you post the emergency phone numbers and make sure to include your name, address, and phone number.

Write down all of your instructions including any pertinent medical information as well as allergy and medication information, bedtimes, and routines.

Make sure your babysitter knows where you keep your toddler's pajamas, if she will need a bath and shampoo, and if you use any powder or lotion.

Show your babysitter how to turn on the television and DVD player as many homes have multiple boxes. There is nothing worse than sitting in silence while her little charge is fast asleep.

If you have a pet, be sure to tell her the pet's routine.

Let the babysitter know you will be calling to check in. But try to keep the calls to a minimum.

Tell her approximately when you will be home and make sure to call if you are running late.

SUCCESS

You call and your toddler is happily snoring away.

When you come in your babysitter can't wait to tell you all about her night with your toddler.

The house is spotless.

She thanks you for the opportunity to care for your toddler.

The next morning your toddler tells you all about her fun night with the babysitter.

THE ABCS OF TODDLER CARE

My mom used to say it doesn't matter how many kids you have because one kid'll take up 100 percent of your time. So more kids can't possibly take up more than 100 percent of your time.

—*Karen Brown*

A good film is when the price of the dinner, theater admission, and the babysitter were worth it.

—*Alfred Hitchcock*

LOVE, LOVE ME DO!

Keeping the Magic in Your Relationship

You really thought once your little one reached toddlerhood you wouldn't be so exhausted. You thought you would have more time to take care of yourself as well as your relationship. And it would be great to look forward to date night each week. You even imagined going away with your hubby for a romantic weekend and leaving little Alison with grandma and grandpa. Oh, yes!

Oh, no! Seriously, it's a good day when you can actually put makeup on and wear something presentable. Those sweats are "oh so comfortable" and who cares what you're wearing when you take Alison into dance class anyway?

Sex? You've got to be kidding. If there is actually a night when your little precious doesn't call you into her room ten times, you are ready to hit the sack the minute those little eyes close and those wonderful sleep sounds radiate from her room. Your husband has to understand. He gets up early, works all day, and helps with your toddler. Isn't he tired too?

So here are the facts—relationships are like flowers. You need to keep that watering can full and ready all the time or the flowers will start to wilt if you ignore them. Yes, it does take some work but keeping life fun and full of surprises while raising a toddler is so important.

Here are some tips to keep the magic alive:

Exercise is a must, even if you only carve out an hour three times a week. It's not only good for your body but also does great things for your mind. And it's fun to work out together.

Plan healthy meals and snacks and keep the junk food out of your house. If it's not there you can't eat it. And it takes too much effort to drive to the store to get your candy fix.

If you both work full-time, go to the grocery store once a week and plan your meals for that week. You can even prepare a few meals and put them in the freezer if you have the time and energy during the weekend.

Divide the household responsibilities between you and your hubby. Having to do it all is a prescription for resentment.

Discuss toddler duty and write the tasks on a whiteboard calendar posted in a visible place. Who will be in charge of baths and when? Who makes your toddler breakfast and takes her to school? Knowing that you will help and support each other is vital to a good parenting relationship.

Give each other a "good morning hug" no matter how tired or rushed you may be. It's a great way to start out the day.

Give each other a kiss when you leave the house and when you return. It's a great habit to make you both feel loved.

Remember to give each other two compliments a day. They're free, easy, and powerful. Creating that warm, fuzzy, and appreciated feeling is so important in any relationship.

When my children were little, I used to go to the grocery store early Sunday morning before the rush. I had a meal book where I wrote down what I would be making for dinner each night during the week and bought all those ingredients on Sunday. The only changes I allowed were switching the nights, not the menus. One trip to the grocery store along with my menu book not only saved me lots of money, but also made my life so much easier.

Make nice... as Bambi's friend Thumper says, "If you can't say somethin' nice, don't say nothin' at all." Once those hurtful words come out of your mouth, you can't take them back.

Choose your battles wisely. Don't take your grumpiness out on your mate. Use the ten-second rule. Count to ten and think about the importance of the issue before the battle begins. Most times you will find it's

Groupon.com is a great site to get discounts on your favorite restaurants and services. Sign up to get phone alerts so you never miss a chance for a fun night out while sticking to your budget.

just not that important.

Write some silly, loving notes and every so often hide them in a funny place. There's not a better pick-me-up during a long hard day.

Stock up on those silly romance cards. Once a week, write a loving message in the card and put one in her underwear drawer or wrapped in his boxers. Laughing is a great stress reliever. So try to keep a sense of humor no matter how hectic your day may be.

Send each other a quick text message each day. Even one sentence will make your hearts smile.

Women love flowers. It's easy to visit the florist, fill out six cards, and prepay for some beauties to be sent to mommy once a month. And don't forget to mark on your calendar when you've scheduled the delivery so you can anticipate the "big thank you!"

Treat daddy to a "surprise lunch." Check to see that he will not be in a lunch meeting and has a clear schedule. Call him to say not to leave his office during the lunch hour and have his favorite restaurant deliver lunch.

Even better, hire a babysitter and show up as the delivery girl. Surprise your hubby with a special picnic lunch that you prepared with all his favorites.

Once a week, plan a late romantic dinner after your toddler is asleep. Write it on your calendar and stick to the plan even if you're tired. Set the table with a tablecloth, candles, cloth napkins, and your best china. (Paper plates work too.) Ask your honey to pick up takeout on his way home. Turn the lights down, light the candles, put on some mellow music, and enjoy each other. Relationships need feeding just like your babies!

Date night once a week is a *must*, even if you just stay home and watch a movie together after your toddler is asleep.

Hire a babysitter the same night each week, put on your fancy clothes, and go out on the town. And no shoptalk, this night is for you and your honey. Toddlers and schedules can wait until tomorrow.

If you're lucky enough to have family members that live near you, ask if they will do an overnight and promise to return the favor. You won't believe what one night away will do for your relationship and your psyche!

Here is a list of some other fun things to do to keep your hearts smiling:

Go out to dinner at your favorite restaurant.

Get takeout from your favorite restaurant.

Go to the movies.

Rent a movie, make some popcorn, and just snuggle on the couch.

Go out with friends.

Go to the mall and buy each other a special present just for being great parents.

Go to a jazz club and pretend it's a first date!

Go dancing. What great exercise and lots of fun!

Go to the ice cream shop and share a banana split without worrying about those calories.

Take a picnic dinner to the park complete with wine and candles.

Go to the bookstore and buy a book that is not about parenting.

Just cuddle until you both fall asleep—for the *entire night!*

THE ABCS OF TODDLER CARE

Love is my decision to make your problem my concern.
—*Robert Schuller*

I truly feel that there are as many ways of loving as there are people in the
world and as there are days in the lives of those people.
—*Dr. Mary Calderone*

"I PROMISE WE WON'T MEDDLE!"

How to Be the Best Grandparents in the World

There is nothing better than being a grandparent. Spending time with your grandchild is better than any gift in the world. And as many grandparents will attest, "you get the best of both worlds." Grandparents play, have fun, and then go home and get a full night's sleep, unlike their daughter or son who may not have that luxury.

But there can be challenges and many times you become the outlaw instead of the in-law! Things such as discipline, naps, staying up late, treats, and gifts are some of the issues that many grandparents struggle with. And yes, you do have lots of experience and great advice, but how do you know when you are crossing that fine line when your pride and joy is in your care?

The following tips should help keep the peace:

If there are two sets of grandparents, choose different names and talk about each grandparent, what they look like, and whose mommy and daddy they are. For example, "I'm Grandma Rose and I have brown hair. Grandma Jo wears glasses." The grandparent concept can be very confusing to a toddler.

While you may want to drop by unannounced for a grandparent fix...*don't!* Talk to your children about setting aside a special afternoon or day that works for everyone's schedule. Showing up during naptime and expecting to wake up little Sara is a big "no no!"

If you call and no one answers, don't assume the worst and don't keep calling or think something may be wrong. Toddlers demand a lot of attention and mommy may not be able to get to the phone.

Try your best *not* to give unsolicited advice even if you're nervous or don't agree with your children's parenting methods. Yes, you mean well and were successful in raising your children, but many things have changed over the years.

If you can't help yourself and do offer advice, back off if it's not well received. We all have to make our own mistakes and it's not worth a fight.

Don't ever override mommy and daddy and try to discipline your grandchild. It's their job so don't butt in.

Ask your child what they would like you to do when your grandchild is in your care and they have a tantrum. Time-out, hugs, walking away, redirection? Having everyone on the same page makes it easier. And consistency is so important.

Try your best to do what your children ask when caring for your grandchildren even if you don't agree. Hard feelings take away from those precious moments.

If you are going to be babysitting for your grandchild, ask mommy to write down all the instructions along with emergency numbers. Having things in writing prevents any misunderstandings.

Ask how to work all those newfangled gadgets in the home. There is nothing more frustrating than not being able to turn on your grandchild's favorite video because you don't know how to work the four television remotes.

Be sure to ask what foods your grandchild can eat and if she has any restrictions. There have been more than a few visits to the emergency room when a well-meaning grandpa unknowingly shared a peanut butter sandwich with their grandchild who was allergic to nuts.

If your grandchild has any allergies, post a sign on the refrigerator so no one forgets.

If your grandchild is not allowed to have sweets, as tempting as it may be, don't think one piece won't hurt with, "This will be our secret!" It is so unfair to put your grandchild in a position to keep something from mommy and daddy.

If you are nervous about any aspect of caring for your grandchild, don't be embarrassed to say so. Ask questions until you are cool, calm, and collected.

If you are spending one-on-one time with your grandchild each week, make a special box of fun. Fill it with arts and crafts, age-appropriate books, games, puzzles, and videos that only the two of you play with when you're together. (Check out the chapter "Mommy, I'm Bored—Fun Toddler Activities.")

Take lots of pictures and make two photo books: one for you and one for your grandchild. Kodak memories are priceless and grandparents love to show pictures and brag about their grandchildren!

If your grandchild will be spending the night at your house, make sure it's not a danger zone. Taking the time to childproof can prevent terrible accidents.

If you have medicine or vitamins sitting on your counter, lock them away and out of reach.

Get in the habit of putting the

Two of my favorite books to share with young grandchildren are *Here Comes Grandma!* by Janet Lord and *How to Babysit a Grandpa* by Jean Reagan and Lee Wildish.

lid down on the toilet or purchase a toilet lock. (Unfortunately, there have been drowning accidents when a toddler fell into the water.)

Purchase doorknob covers so your grandchild can't get into unsafe rooms.

If you have computer cords or anything else attached to the wall with pushpins, make them high enough that your grandchild can't reach.

Purchase covers for your stove knobs.

If you have a gas fireplace, remove the jet key.

Be sure your bookshelves are securely anchored to the wall. Toddlers like to climb and accidents happen in the blink of an eye.

If you save coins and they're sitting in an open jar, put it away. Shiny money will go right into the mouth.

If you have a pool, make sure the gate is locked or you have a childproof door a toddler can't open.

Invest in a pool alarm; it's well worth the money.

Keep your pet's food out of reach.

Keep a well-stocked first aid kit within reach as well as your emergency numbers posted in clear view (not in a book or a drawer).

Keep a bottle of ipecac syrup but never use it until you talk to Poison Control or a physician. The phone number for the National Poison Hotline is 800-222-1222.

I know one grandma that had a box of props to use during their Skype visits. She put on puppet shows, made stuffed animals talk, and read books to her granddaughter.

If you have special keepsakes, art, or any breakables within your

grandchild's reach, put them away. It's easier than saying "Don't touch" over and over. Toddlers are curious about everything.

Make sure you and grandpa always know which one of you is watching your grandchild. Don't ever assume it's the other one.

LONG-DISTANCE GRANDPARENTING

Send your grandchild a special picture of you and grandpa so she knows who you are.

Another grandma told me she schedules a Skype tea party with her three-year-old each Saturday. Grandma had cookies and tea at her table and her granddaughter had her own tea party set-up 2500 miles away. They would each take bites and sips and pretended to give some to each other. To hear "Yum" through the computer is worth its weight in gold!

Ask mommy or daddy to set up a certain day and time to call and talk to your grandchild. They know best when she will not be napping, tired, hungry, or cranky. But keep an open mind, as every day can be different in a toddler's life.

Do not call if you are having a bad storm in your area. Getting cut off or having lots of static is not a good mix for connecting.

If you're computer savvy and use Skype, get ready to have some fun. The computer is like a television to a toddler.

Ask your grandchild to show you her toys, pictures, or anything else she wants to share while you're Skyping. The sky is the limit!

Even if your grandchild is too little to carry on a conversation, let her hear your voice.

Sing a special song each time you call and ask her to sing along. Pick an age-appropriate song. Most young toddlers know "Baa Baa Black Sheep."

Don't get upset if your grandchild only listens or talks for a few minutes. It's not personal. Having

Here are two great feel-good books for grandparents to read: *Why I Love Grandma: 100 Reasons* by Gregory E. and Meagan Lang and *Chicken Soup for the Grandparent's Soul* by Jack Canfield. Grandparents.com is a great site to visit.

a long attention span is not a strong suit with toddlers. Just go with the flow and don't get upset if the call doesn't go as you planned. Try to be flexible and forgiving.

Have fun and enjoy being a grandparent! There's nothing better!

THE ABCS OF TODDLER CARE

Grandmas are moms with lots of frosting.
—Author Unknown

A grandfather is someone with silver in his hair and gold in his heart.
—Author Unknown

Grandchildren don't stay young forever, which is good because Pop-pops
have only so many horsey rides in them.
—Gene Perret

When your mother asks, "Do you want a piece of advice?" it is a mere
formality. It doesn't matter if you answer yes or no. You're going to get it
anyway.
—Erma Bombeck

COOKS AND BOOKS

There is nothing better than whipping up a fun recipe with your toddler and sharing a book about her creation! Here are some fun and easy recipes along with books to match each one. You never know how many famous chefs or authors have been born from these early cooking and reading experiences!

BAGEL FACES

Bagels

1 small package cream cheese

Cherry tomatoes

Black olives

Sprouts

Cucumbers (cut into rounds)

Carrots (cut into rounds)

Red peppers (cut into thin strips)

Give your toddler a paper plate with the following:

2 Tbsp. cream cheese

1 cherry tomato

2 black olives

Few sprouts (for hair, mustache, beard)

2 cucumber rounds

2 carrot rounds

1 red pepper strip

1 plastic knife

Ask her to spread a thin layer of cream cheese on the bagel. Then make a face using the vegetables.

All About Faces by La ZOO is a great book to read with this recipe.

FRUIT KABOBS WITH MARSHMALLOW FACES

1 package of wooden skewers

Food coloring (assorted colors)

Toothpicks

Banana (cut in thick rounds)

Apples (cut in two-inch pieces)

Grapes

Marshmallows (regular size)

Give your toddler a paper plate with the following:

4 pieces banana

4 pieces apple

4 grapes

2 marshmallows

On a smaller paper plate, put the following:

4 toothpicks

2–3 drops each color of food coloring

Dip one end of the toothpick in the food coloring and make a face on the marshmallows by dotting it with the toothpick.

Then thread the fruit and marshmallows on the skewers.

Glad Monster, Sad Monster by Ed Emberley is the perfect book to read while you enjoy your Fruit Kabobs.

FIELD OF GREENS

1 package crescent rolls (4 oz.)

1 small package cream cheese

Alfalfa sprouts

Green or red peppers (cut into one-inch strips)

Zucchini (cut into quarter-inch rounds)

Carrots (cut into quarter-inch rounds)

Broccoli trees (one inch in length)

Spray 10 x 13 cookie sheet with cooking spray.

Press the crescent rolls into large square on cookie sheet.

Bake at 375 degrees for 8–10 minutes until golden. (Mommy does this step.)

Place the baked crescent rolls on a square platter to cool.

When the square is cool, spread with small amount of cream cheese.

Place vegetables on top in rows to look like a field.

Barnyard Dance by Sandra Boynton will have your toddler laughing out loud!

THE EDIBLE RACECAR

1 six-inch hoagie bun (don't use hot dog rolls, they are too soft, Kaiser rolls work better)

1 cup sour cream

1 package of dip (any flavor will work)

1 small package of cream cheese

1 cucumber (cut in half-inch rounds)

1 carrot (cut in half-inch rounds)

1 jar sliced, green, pimento-filled olives

1 can sliced black olives

Red pepper (cut in strips)

Broccoli (cut in small trees, about 3–4 inches in length)

Baby carrots

Celery sticks

Carefully scoop out center of roll, leaving bottom intact. (Mommy should do this.)

Make the dip according to directions with your toddler doing the mixing and pouring.

Give her a plate with the following:

Scooped-out bun, paper cup containing about a quarter cup of dip, 1 tablespoon cream cheese, 4 cucumber rounds, 4 carrot rounds, 2 green olive slices, 2 black olive slices, pepper strip, broccoli tree, baby carrot, celery stick, 1 straw, plastic spoon and knife.

Fill scooped-out roll with dip.

Make a hole in the center of each cucumber round with a straw and place carrot round in the hole using a little cream cheese for the glue. Spread a tiny amount of cream cheese on one side of the cucumber for the glue. Stick one cucumber axle on each side of the car for the wheels.

Put two tiny dabs of cream cheese on the front of the roll. Place the black olive on the cream cheese and put the green olive inside. These are the headlights.

Fill the car with the remaining vegetables.

The Racecar Alphabet by Brian Floca will have your toddler whirring around the room!

PRETEND SOUP

2 cups orange juice

One-half cup plain yogurt

1 Tbsp. honey

2 tsp. lemon juice

1 small banana, sliced

1 cup blueberries, strawberries, and/or raspberries

Using a measuring cup, let your toddler pour all the above ingredients except the fruit into a bowl. Using a wire whisk, have her mix until combined and smooth.

Put 3–4 banana slices and some berries in the bottom of a small bowl.

Ladle the soup over the fruit.

You can float goldfish grahams on top if desired.

Dragon's Alphabet Soup by Rachel Yu, Michael Yu, and Kayleigh Scheidt is great to read with this recipe.

CIRCUS PUDDING

1 box instant pudding (any flavor desired)

2 cups milk

Animal crackers, teddy grahams, circus animals, etc.

Plastic bowl

Plastic measuring cup

Big spoon

Ladle

Clear plastic disposable cups

Prepare pudding as directed on package, with your toddler doing the pouring and mixing. Then have her ladle the pudding into the cups. Decorate top with animal crackers, teddy grahams, and circus animals.

You can also make "dirt cups" by crushing chocolate cookies into crumbs, sprinkling them on top of the pudding, and pushing a gummy worm on the top. Toddler boys especially love this one!

Thomas Goes to the Circus by Josie Yee and *Diary of a Worm* by Doreen Cronin are fun books to share.

FUN ANIMAL STICKS

    Celery (cut into six-inch stalks, leaves removed)

    1 small package of cream cheese

    Ritz cracker crumbs

    Goldfish shaped crackers

Give your toddler a paper plate with the following:

    1 celery stalk

    1 Tbsp. cream cheese

    1 Tbsp. Ritz cracker crumbs

    8–10 goldfish crackers

    Plastic knife

Ask your toddler to fill the middle of the celery with cream cheese, by using the plastic knife.

Top with cracker crumbs.

Put goldfish in a row on top of mixture like they are swimming.

Read a story together about the sea and enjoy your treat. You can also use raisins for ants if you want this recipe to be about insects.

Dear Zoo by Rod Campbell and *Bugs! Bugs! Bugs!* by Bob Barner will bring lots of giggles.

LITTLE HOUSE IN THE WOODS

2 graham cracker squares

1 can of icing (any flavor desired)

Edible decorations: raisins, pretzel sticks, M&M's, gummy bears, etc.

Take one graham square and frost with a medium layer of icing (this will be the glue as well as the paint).

Take the other graham square and break it in half vertically. Put a small amount of icing on the tops and bottoms of each half and lay on top of the house diagonally, with the tops touching, to form the roof (like a half triangle).

Decorate the house by gently sticking the edible decorations to the iced roof.

Make up a fun story about your house or read Stan and Jan Berenstain's book, *The Berenstain Bears' Moving Day.*

THE TEDDY BEAR'S PICNIC (FOR TODDLERS WITHOUT NUT ALLERGIES)

1 cup of peanut butter or any kind of nut butter

1 cup instant dry milk

1 Tbsp. honey

Raisins

Hershey's Kiss

Mini M&M's

Food coloring (any color but yellow as it won't show up)

Toothpicks

Mix peanut butter and milk together.

Add honey into mixture until pliable dough forms. Add more milk if the dough is too sticky.

Give your toddler a paper plate with the following:

2 Tbsp. dough

1 raisin

2 M&M's

1 Hershey's Kiss

1 toothpick

2 drops food coloring (blue or red)

Give your toddler a tablespoon of dough to roll into a ball for the body.

Then give her a teaspoon of dough to roll into a smaller ball for the head.

Gently push the small ball on top of the larger ball but hard enough so it doesn't fall off.

Dip the end of the toothpick into food coloring and gently push into the top ball of dough to make dots for eyes, nose, and mouth.

Take a tiny pinch of dough and stick to each side of the head for ears.

Put a Hershey's Kiss on top of head for a hat.

Use the raisin or M&M's for the belly button or buttons.

You can also use this dough to make a bunny. Instead of pressing dough to the sides of head, make two bunny ears and press on top.

Teddy Bears' Picnic by Jimmy Kennedy and Alexandra Day is the perfect book to read with this recipe.

A PINK DIP

1 carton raspberries (thaw and drain if using frozen)

1 small package cream cheese

1 cup vanilla yogurt

2 tsp. lemon juice

Apple wedges for dipping

Pear wedges for dipping

Strawberries for dipping

Ask your toddler to pour the raspberries into a food processor or blender. Then have her add the cream cheese and ask her to press the button to blend until smooth. Pour mixture into a bowl and let her whisk in the yogurt and lemon juice to make it pink.

Ladle mixture into a cup or small bowl.

Talk about things that are pink while dipping the fruit. (You can also dip pretzels, marshmallows, and grahams.)

Little Elmo's Book of Colors by Norman Gorbaty is a fun way for your toddler to learn her colors.

THE COLOR RED

1 carton fresh strawberries or raspberries (frozen without syrup will work too)

1 pound cake (cut into two-inch squares)

Just fruit strawberry or raspberry jam

1 carton Cool Whip

Give your toddler a paper plate and a plastic knife or spreader, 4 squares of pound cake, 1 teaspoon of jam, 5 strawberries or raspberries, and 3 table-spoons of Cool Whip.

Ask your toddler to spread the top of each square with a small amount of jam and put the two squares together like a sandwich.

Have her spoon the berries and the Cool Whip on top of the pound cake sandwich.

Read *The Little Red Caboose* by Marian Potter and Tibor Gergely and talk about all the things that are red.

LEMON LIME BUBBLES

2 Tbsp. lemon juice

2 Tbsp. lime juice

One-quarter cup plus 2 Tbsp. apple juice concentrate (thawed)

1 cup unflavored club soda

Give your toddler a clear plastic cup, half a lemon, half a lime.

Ask her to squeeze the juice into the cup.

Then let her pour in the apple juice and gently mix with a plastic spoon.

Pour in the club soda last and stir gently to make the bubbles.

Clifford Counts Bubbles by Norman Bridwell is fun to read while enjoying your special drink.

MAGIC WANDS

Pretzel rods

One-half cup white chocolate chips

One-half cup semisweet chocolate chips

2 tsp. cooking oil

Edible decorations: sprinkles, coconut, raisins, M&M's, etc.

Let your toddler measure and pour the white and semisweet chocolate chips in two separate microwave-safe bowls. (Mommy needs to do this part.) Melt the chips in the microwave at one-minute intervals until done. (Chocolate melts fast.)

When melted, add a quarter teaspoon cooking oil to each bowl and mix until smooth. Make sure the bowl is not hot to the touch if your toddler will be doing this step.

Show your toddler how to dip one end of the pretzel rod into the chocolate mixture and then into the decorations.

Put on waxed paper and place in refrigerator for 15 minutes to dry.

Strega Nona's Magic Lessons by Tomie dePaola is a fun book to read with older toddlers.

CANDY SUSHI

Rice Krispie treats
Fruit roll-ups
Swedish Fish

Cut Rice Krispie bar into two-inch squares. Roll into a log. Place Swedish Fish on top and wrap an eighth-inch wide piece of fruit roll-up around with two ends coming together on the underside.

For another shape: roll each piece of Rice Krispie into a round disk. Wrap an eighth-inch wide piece of fruit roll-up around outside of disk. Top with Swedish Fish and tiny balls of fruit roll-ups.

I love *First Book of Sushi* by Amy Wilson Sanger.

These recipes are not only fun to make and delicious to eat, but also are great small motor activities for those little hands.

THE ABCS OF TODDLER CARE

In general my children refuse to eat anything that hasn't
danced on television.
—*Erma Bombeck*

Children are made readers on the laps of their parents.
—*Emilie Buchwald*

"MOMMY, I'M BORED!"

Fun Toddler Activities

There is nothing worse than hearing your toddler whine and follow you around the house because she thinks she has nothing to do. You are ready to pull your hair out in frustration. As you look around her playroom, you just don't get it. There are so many toys, books, and puzzles. How can your toddler possibly be bored? But she is, and you've run out of ideas to keep her occupied.

Here are some fun and easy activities to make that whining disappear:

The Mall Walker—The mall can be a fun adventure. Start your journey at the food court for some breakfast or lunch. Walk down to the pet store, stopping along the way to window-shop. When you get to the pet store, let mommy ask if you can take one of the puppies into their special playroom and get acquainted. Continue your journey through the mall looking in the hobby shop window to see if the train is running today and pretend you're the engineer. Next stop is the indoor playground. Take off your shoes and have a ball. Finally finish your outing with a stop for some frozen yogurt. What a fun day as well as a great and inexpensive way to stay out of the heat if it's summertime.

It's Movie Time—Plan a movie date. Either rent a video or go out to the movies. Many movie theaters have special children's days for a discounted price during the summer and holidays. Let your toddler put together a special snack bag with pretzels, goldfish, raisins, and M&M's and don't forget to take a bottle of water along and her favorite blanket.

Playground Pajama Party—Take your toddler to the playground in her pj's first thing in the morning. Then go out to breakfast.

Miniature Gardener—Fill a spray bottle with water and ask your toddler to water the plants. You can also purchase a miniature watering can for those outside flowers. And if you fill a small plastic bowl with water, when the spray bottle is empty, your toddler can fill it all by herself. Make sure not to fill up a bucket, as there have been many accidents with toddlers falling into a bucket of water headfirst.

Take your toddler to the store and let her pick out a small plant or herb to put in her own special flowerpot. Teach her how to water and take care of it each day. Trader Joe's is a wonderful place to go for inexpensive herb plants. I love their basil plants.

Do You Need a Painter?—Go to the dollar store and buy a spray bottle, some paintbrushes, a watering can, and some sponges. Put water in the spray bottle and watering can. Dress your toddler in her bathing suit, take her outside, and let her paint the house. What fun!

Little Landscaper—When you are doing yard work, give your toddler a small cardboard box and attach a short rope. She'll love collecting the clippings to take to your compost pile. Just be sure your sharp clippers are out of her reach.

Chalk Writing—Purchase a miniature chalkboard, some chalk, and an eraser and let your toddler draw to her heart's content. (You can find these at the dollar store.) You can also purchase a box of outside chalk to use on the sidewalk. Show her how to spray the chalk drawings with water to mix the colors together or wash them all away.

The Cleanup Woman—Toddlers love to help with chores. Give your little helper a paper towel or a clean rag and let her dust away. (Younger toddlers love this one!)

When it's laundry time, ask your toddler to help you by picking out all the clothes that are a certain color and put them in the washer or dryer. What a fun way to learn her colors.

It's Story Time—Look in your local newspaper or online to see if any libraries or bookstores have children's story times. And don't forget to pick out a book or two to read at home.

You can also order books from many Internet sites such as www. Audible.com and listen to a story together. An added plus is that you can stop and start the story at any time if you want to talk about it with your toddler, if it's naptime, or if you both just need a break.

Arts and Crafts—Crayola has wonderful arts and crafts projects. One of my favorite Crayola activities is finger-painting. The box comes complete with special paper so the paint will only color the paper and not your toddler or the carpet.

Toddlers love to make collages. Give your toddler a piece of construction paper, a glue stick, and some different shaped pasta, buttons, yarn, fabric, markers, and any other fun arts and crafts supplies you may have on hand. Show her how to glue them onto the paper to make a beautiful collage. And remember, it's her masterpiece so don't be tempted to tell your toddler where to glue anything.

It's Fun to Make Jewelry—Purchase some different shaped pasta with holes large enough for a piece of yarn to go through and some colorful yarn. (Trader Joe's is a great place to purchase fun-shaped pasta.) Measure a piece of yarn long enough to fit over your toddler's head or around her wrist that will fit loosely when you tie the ends together.

To make a bracelet or necklace do the following (mommy's part first): Take one piece of pasta and pull one end of the yarn through the hole to make a knot so it doesn't slip off. Then show your toddler how to string each piece of pasta on the yarn. When she's finished stringing, tie the two ends together.

If you purchase white pasta and want to color it, try this: Place the pasta in a small plastic baggie, add a few drops of food coloring, seal the bag tightly, and shake until you get the desired color. Spread the pasta out on a paper plate to dry. It should be ready to use in a few hours. Your toddler can help with the shaking part.

My Little Florist (this one takes a few steps)—You will need a glue stick, yarn, buttons or uncooked pasta, construction paper, wooden Popsicle sticks, crayons or markers, a small terra-cotta flowerpot, and a small circle of Styrofoam to fit in the flowerpot. Target, Michaels, and Wal-Mart have all these items available. Put a piece of construction paper on the floor and ask your toddler to stand on it without shoes and socks so you can trace her feet. Put two pieces of construction paper together or fold one piece in half so you have four traced feet. Cut them out for her. Then have your toddler decorate her feet with crayons, markers, buttons, yarn, etc. Glue one paper foot at the heel end on each Popsicle stick. You will have four Popsicle stick feet. Place the piece of Styrofoam in the flowerpot and have your toddler push each Popsicle stick into the Styrofoam. Voila…you have a beautiful flowerpot and keepsake. If you want leaves, cut some from green construction paper and glue them onto the Popsicle sticks. If you want to cover the Styrofoam, put Hershey's Kisses, buttons, or wrapped candy on top. And don't forget to write the date and your toddler's age on the bottom of the flowerpot. What a great memory to have in years to come.

My Little Chef—Toddlers love to bake cookies. If you don't want to make the dough from scratch, purchase the prepared sugar cookie mix from the grocery store. With cookie cutters, show your toddler how to cut out the shapes. Let your little chef decorate the cutout dough with M&Ms, raisins, sprinkles, or dried fruit. Bake them per your recipe's directions.

You can make cookie pops by gently sticking a Popsicle stick halfway up the dough on the cookie sheet before baking.

To make special Popsicle treats purchase some small paper cups and place them on a cookie sheet. Give your toddler some cherries or grapes to put in the bottom of each paper cup. Pour some fruit juice or juice water (a quarter juice with three-quarters water) into a measuring cup. Then ask your toddler to pour this liquid into a small paper cup filling it almost to the top. Put a Popsicle stick in the middle of each cup and freeze for three to four hours. This is a great morning activity that will be ready as a special afternoon treat!

Make a yogurt "sundae bar." Fill three small paper cups with raisins, cut-up fresh fruit, and cereal. Get out the ice cream scoop and show your toddler how to scoop frozen yogurt into a small dish. Then let her mix in the condiments. You can add some whipped cream and a strawberry on top if desired. What a fun and healthy treat! (You can also use regular yogurt in place of the frozen yogurt.)

Plan a special indoor picnic and prepare the feast together. Use a cookie cutter to make fun bread shapes for your sandwiches. Turkey, cheese, and tuna are some good choices. Instead of chips serve carrot disks, celery sticks, and cucumber rounds. Make a dip using plain yogurt or ranch dressing. For a special drink, mix fruit juice with a little club soda and serve in a festive cup with an orange slice on the rim. Spread a blanket on the floor and enjoy your indoor adventure.

Pudding painting is easy and fun. Give your toddler a package of instant pudding to pour into a plastic bowl. Put the milk into a measuring cup and let her pour it into the pudding bowl. Give her a big spoon to mix the pudding until it thickens. Next give your toddler a paper plate, some sprinkles, raisins, and animal crackers, or cereal. Put a small amount of pudding on the paper plate and tell her "no spoons"…finger-painting time. Toddlers love to sprinkle; use the animal crackers as a dip and the raisins as eyes if she is making a pudding face. Sometimes playing with food is allowed.

Babysitters Are Fun—Hire a high school student to come to your house one or two times a week. Save a special activity for the two of them to do on these days. Whether it's arts and crafts, baking, or doing puzzles together, it's a fun time for your toddler and a break for you.

Old Can Be New—Remember to rotate your toddler's toys each month. Seeing a favorite toy they haven't played with in a long time is a fun surprise!

Planning ahead is the recipe for lots of giggles and fun. And don't be afraid to be creative. Add your own activities to the list and enjoy these happy times with your toddler.

THE ABCS OF TODDLER CARE

Make a special arts and crafts box for your empty egg cartons, buttons, yarn, plastic water bottles, and any other empties that are ready for the trash. You'll be surprised at how many throwaways make great toddler art projects.

—*Pat W., Pennsylvania*

Sharpen both ends of your toddler's crayons with a special sharpener; she won't get upset if one end breaks and she won't have to figure out which end to use.

—*Pat W., New Jersey*

I designate a kitchen cabinet that's low enough for my toddler to reach. When we come home from the grocery store, she knows it's her job to put the cereal, rice, and pasta in this cabinet. Toddlers love to help!

—*JoAnn O., Arizona*

If you want children to keep their feet on the ground, put some responsibility on their shoulders.

—*Abigail Van Buren*

A LITTLE OF THIS AND THAT

If your toddler doesn't like cooked vegetables, offer her raw vegetables with ranch dressing as a dip. Toddlers love dipping.

If your toddler doesn't like any vegetables, you can sneak them into pasta sauce, soups, eggs, and even smoothies. Or buy vegetable juice (carrot, tomato, etc.), pour it into a blender with some ice, and give it a funny name. Tell your toddler that the "Orange Monster Milkshake" will make him big and strong!

My son loves pizza but hates vegetables. I make my own by using a whole wheat muffin, sneaking the vegetables under the cheese, and letting him decorate the pizza with his favorites, pineapple and black olives.

—Andrea R.

You can't force toddlers to eat. And the more you draw attention to their non-eating, the more power you give them. Let it go. Your toddler will eat when she is hungry. I promise she won't starve.

If there are foods your toddler doesn't like, continue to offer them along with some of her favorites. One bite and she may be hooked.

If there is a certain food you don't like, keep it to yourself. Toddlers love to copy mommy. Everyone's tastes are different and it could become her new favorite.

If your toddler is not a big eater, don't turn her into a grazer by offering sugary snacks throughout the day to make up for meals. If she gets hungry enough she will eat at mealtimes. *French Kids Eat Everything* by Karen Le Billon is a great book to get your toddlers on track with healthy eating.

When my son was a toddler, he hated his socks. I would put them on and he would cry and say there was a line on the bottom. I bought white tube socks. And while they almost came up to his knees, no more tears.

My toddler had the worst time learning to tie his shoes. We struggled each day until I found a great shoe-tying kit called "One, Two, Tie My Shoe," created by Mendy K. Hassen. Check out her website to order the kit: www.onetwotiemyshoe.com.

One grandma shared a great tip for her bored grandchildren. It was an hour before dinner and they were bored and cranky. She knew she would be leaving on a business trip the next day so she asked them to do an art project that she could take with her and display for everyone to see. They immediately got their paper, markers, glue sticks, and collage materials and started making their masterpieces. And grandma was so proud to share these priceless pictures with all her coworkers.

—Joan M.

If your toddler wakes up from her nap on the wrong side of the bed, cranky and clingy, choose one of her favorite books and start to read it aloud. Before you know it your toddler will be cuddled in your lap.

—Joan M.

Use different voices when reading to your toddler and get ready for lots of giggles.

Many toddlers learn to read by using sounds. Starting with easy three-letter words like eat, run, sit, and nap. Practice five minutes a day.

—Nick D.

Read, read, and read to your toddlers, stories, recipes, items on the grocery shelves as it teaches them to associate letters/words and sounds. When you read a story to your toddler, engage them in the story by asking what comes next. And then ask your toddler to read a favorite book to you even if they don't know the exact words. Learning can be fun.

—Robin B.

When you're having a family conversation, try to include your toddler. It will teach her interacting skills that are polite and thoughtful. No one likes to feel left out no matter what age.

—Robin B.

By the time your toddler is four years old she should know her first and last name and phone number. Practice this each day until she has it down pat. You never know when it will come in handy.

Talk to your older (3–4 years old) toddler about "stranger danger." Make it age-appropriate, factual but not scary. Then choose a special private word that your toddler, mommy, and daddy know and explain when the three of you will use this word.

Teach your toddler how to politely answer the phone and immediately give it to you or daddy unless she knows it's a family member. You don't want her talking to a stranger (telemarketer) or anyone else. Remember that toddlers tell all and don't discriminate.

When dressing your toddler, think about comfort. Those clunky Nike sneakers or a tight skirt can hinder her movement. Forget the fashion statement.

—Robin B.

If your toddler goes to a preschool with sand on the playground, place a bucket outside your door and have him empty his shoes before he comes in the house.

—Jennifer H.

Buying gently used toddler clothing at garage sales will save you lots of money. And you won't have to worry if they get dirty or torn.

—Robin B.

If you can't get your toddler to hold still while you put sunscreen on her, sing the "Hokey Pokey" while applying it. Not only does this make it fun, but it also helps your toddler learn left from right.

—Teresamme R.

If you have lots of errands to run, plan a time when you don't have to take your toddler. There is nothing more tiring than having to take your toddler in and out of her car seat when she's grumpy and tired. One or two errands are fine, but more than that, plan ahead.

After a trip to the grocery store, there were always lots of bags to unload. I made sure to have the grocery clerk make a few bags really light so my toddler could help mommy carry in the groceries.

> *When we got home from the grocery store, we always taught our impatient toddler to place both his hands on the car while I unloaded the groceries. It gave him something special to do and I could watch him and know he was safe.*
>
> *—Marty R*

When doing the laundry, ask your toddler to help you put the wet clothes in the dryer. Teach her the colors as you hand her each item. Say, "Here is the blue shirt and here are the red socks." Then ask her to tell you what color an item is. This is a clever but fun way to get two jobs done at once.

If you can't get your toddler to do something, be a good role model and show her how it's done. For example, if your child is too rough with another child at a playdate, demonstrate the behavior you want. Say, "Let's hug Emma softly." Then take your child's arms and guide her into a gentle hug. Or if you have a hard time getting your toddler to brush her teeth, make it a nightly routine you do together, says Penny Donnenfeld, Ph.D.

If your toddler is having a full-blown crying tantrum, try whispering in her ear. Many times this is just enough to stop the tears. Then a big hug is in order.

Ask your toddler to tell you a joke. It will usually be something for the scrapbook as toddlers have a great sense of humor.

Remember to keep your sense of humor too. Raising a toddler can sometimes be a challenge. But there is nothing better than sharing some giggles with your little one while teaching her about the world.

TODDLERS SAY THE DARNDEST THINGS!

In the toddler world, inhibitions don't exist. Toddlers will do whatever strikes them, with no embarrassment and no insecurities, just pure honesty and fun. And there is nothing better than watching your little comedians as they try to conquer the world. Be sure to have your video camera charged and ready at all times!

My toddler son asked, "Mommy, if you're English before you go potty, do you know what are you when you're going potty? European!"

—Blythe L.

Early one morning my husband and I were having breakfast when our toddler walked into the kitchen and announced that she didn't have any more clean underwear. My husband told her he had plenty and she was welcome to borrow a pair of his. Without missing a beat she looked up at him and said, "No thank you, Daddy, that would give me a big butt!"

—Sandy F.

One day when I took my two grandchildren to the park, I noticed little Brennan crossing his legs like he had to go potty, but he insisted he didn't. After we had been there for a bit I noticed another mother laughing hysterically. There's Brennan with his shorts pulled down, peeing on the lawn without a care in the world. He finished his deed, pulled his shorts up, and off he went to play. Ahh...the innocence of toddlers.

—Hyla A.

Four-year-old Jordan had a temper tantrum every morning no matter what outfit she picked out the night before. Finally after the fourth morning, mommy was at her wits' end. She told Jordan she could wear what she had picked out or she would have to go to preschool naked. Jordan got in the car naked. When they arrived at school there was no way she was getting out of the car without clothes. Luckily mommy brought along the clothes she had picked out the night before. One look out the car window and those clothes were on faster than you could blink!

—Randy R.

Grammie was going to care for my two toddlers while I went to work. It was still winter-coat season in New England. I had my children dressed and ready to go. In the time it took me to walk into the bathroom and turn off the light, my daughter had stripped down to her underpants informing me that she was not wearing the outfit I picked out. Knowing I would be late for work I grabbed three outfits from the laundry basket, put her snowsuit on over her underpants, and put her in the car. She had a meltdown all the way to Grammie's house. Once this Grammie listened to her tale about her "mean mother," she got dressed without another peep. Good thing that "mean mother" brought along three outfits! A mother's mantra..."Leave extra time and be flexible and prepared!"

—Robin B.

Toddlers take everything literally. I was filling bottles from a large can of Similac for a weeklong trip. I handed the empty can to three-year-old Kristopher and asked him to "please throw it out." As we piled into the car and drove away looking at our perfectly manicured yard, there was the empty can of Similac, sitting right in the middle of the lawn. When I asked Kristopher why he didn't throw the can in the garbage, he said, "Because you told me to throw it out!" Be careful what you say.

—Joanne K.

My seventeen-month-old got into the habit of kissing herself when she looked in the mirror. One day I took her to see a neighbor. He had just finished waxing his beautiful black car. It was so shiny and spot free. But the minute my toddler saw her reflection she ran as fast as her little legs would carry her and gave the shiny car a big, smeary, wet kiss! While my neighbor was hysterically laughing I wanted to crawl into the nearest hole!

—Amy G.

One day I was taking three-year-old Jordan to McDonalds for lunch. I knew if she took her purse into the restaurant it would be one more thing I would have to carry. As I turned off the car, I said, "You can take your purse into McDonalds but I am not going to carry it." At which she promptly replied, "I didn't intend to take my purse into McDonalds. I need my hands free to eat my hangeber and srench shries!"

—Blythe L.

My four-year-old son Jalen was having "library time" while I was doing paperwork, when he sneezed. I was so into what I was doing I hadn't even noticed. So he says, "Isn't anyone going to say bless you?" I said, "I'm sorry, bless you, Jalen." He says, "Thank you, I owe you one."

—Tiffani F.

I thought I was the smartest young mother in the world when I would tell my two- and four-year-old that if they finished their meal they could have something really special...milk water! I didn't want to see anything go to waste. So the minute they drained their glass of milk, I would reward them by filling it up with water! And I would sound so super-excited when saying, "Finish your lunch so you can have milk water!" It didn't take too long for my brilliant four-year-old to figure out this scheme, and milk water went down the drain!

—Jill M.

When my three-year-old son Jacob got a cut on his finger, I asked if I could put a Band-Aid over it so that it wouldn't get irritated. He replied, "But Mommy, it's not 'earitated,' it's 'fingertated.'"

—Tammi G.

I am a preschool teacher and our kids were eating breakfast one morning and discussing where they were born. One little boy said he was born at Sacred Heart, and a little girl sitting next to him said, "I was born at Sacred Heart too." The little boy turned to her, very concerned, and said, "Really? I didn't see you there."

—Vicki J.

One day my four-year-old daughter Karlyn asked me if she was in my tummy when she was a baby. I told her yes, she then asked me if her brother Wyatt (who was then three) was in my tummy too. I said yes he was. Then she said, "Well, I was line leader!"

—Jill

When the twins were barely two they had just figured how to get themselves undressed and loved running around naked and loved rap music. One morning a very young cable guy was at our house setting up our cable. The twins were in their room and it was a little too quiet. Just as I went to check on them, the cable guy turned on the TV and on came a rap song. All of a sudden, here come my toddlers, naked as the day they were born, dancing and shaking their booties like wild animals! I was so embarrassed! I told them to go put their clothes on immediately, to which they replied, "We can't, we WUB nakey," and kept dancing and giggling. The look on the cable guy's face was priceless! He'll probably never have children!

—Anonymous

One Sunday I was in church with my three-year-old. While we were supposed to be quietly praying, he asked if he could go to the bathroom. I asked him if he could wait a bit as the service was almost over. A moment passed then he decided to loudly tell the entire parish that he had to go now because he was constipated and the fiber was working! Talk about wanting to bury my head in the Bible!

—Anonymous

AND FINALLY, THE PERFECT ENDING TO THIS CHAPTER

A preschool student told his teacher he'd found a cat.

She asked him if it was dead or alive.

"Dead," she was informed.

"How do you know?" asked the teacher.

"Because I pissed in its ear and it didn't move," answered the child innocently.

"You did *what?*" the teacher exclaimed in surprise.

"You know," explained the boy, "I leaned over and went 'Psst!' And it didn't move."

DID YOU KNOW?

Toddler Trivia

Fifty years ago baby bottles were glass and they had to be boiled each time before filling them. Many parents have gone back to using glass bottles today, as they are deemed safer. Many plastic bottles have been made with a chemical called Bisphenol A (BPA), a toxic chemical.

Diapers were either sewn or you purchased them and they were very expensive. The soiled diapers went right into the toilet to soak until mom rinsed it out. Of course no one but mom would do that "icky" job. And if you only had one bathroom, that could be a real problem.

Again, old is new again as many parents use cloth diapers deeming them less expensive and better for the environment. However, today there are diaper services that pick up the soiled diapers and exchange them for clean diapers.

Cloth diapers were first mass-produced by Maria Allen in 1887.

The first disposable diaper was invented by Valerie Hunter-Gordon (née de Ferranti), granddaughter of inventor Sebastian Ziani de Ferranti, in 1947.

When relatives came to visit, there weren't any extra cribs or bassinets. The baby just slept in one of the dresser drawers.

There was no time-out years ago. Switches and paddles were used when a toddler misbehaved. Ouch!

The first public preschool program began at the Franklin School in Chicago in 1925 with the support of the Chicago Women's Club.

For years preschools didn't have computers. They got along just fine with books, puzzles, crayons, glue sticks, and paper.

When I was a baby my grandma used to put me in a basket and put it on the floor of the car when she was driving.

Lots of white bread was served as a snack. Moms used to cut off the crusts and call it "angel food cake."

When my great great aunt was born, she was so little she would fit in her mother's palm. They didn't think she was going to live so the doctor told her mother to keep her in the oven in a loaf pan padded with potholders to keep her warm in the old drafty farmhouse. She lived to be ninety-six, outliving all her brothers and sisters. Her mother's slogan..."We Baked You To Perfection!"

Toddler hearing is better than adult hearing. Hearing in toddlers is often spot-on—toddler ears are so new, they can hear very high frequencies, sounds that older ears have tuned out or can no longer pick up thanks to aging and noise pollution. So although what you tell him to do goes in one toddler ear and out the other, it's not that he's not hearing well: He's most likely hearing your voice—and everything else around him—loud and clear (www.whattoexpect.com).

Toddler ears are shaped differently than adult ears. They may look like little versions of adult ears on the outside, but inside is a whole different story—little ones' canals are narrower and curvier than their grown-up counterparts. That can be a problem for some: Fluid behind the eardrum (from the zillions of colds that toddlers get) can't drain, which can lead to muffled hearing in toddlers and painful ear infections. The good news: As kids grow, those canals widen and straighten for better drainage—meaning fewer chances to develop an ear infection (www.whattoexpect.com).

Experts at Growing Up Milk have found that the average toddler expends the same energy each day as if an adult did 249 minutes in the boxing ring, ran thirty miles, or cycled eighty-two miles at 12–14 mph.

The survey, called First Steps Research, highlights how a toddler's daily antics, including running around, playing in a sandpit, climbing stairs, and playing in a play park, are the same as adults climbing 2,980 meters—twice the height of Ben Nevis, the UK's highest mountain, which stands at 1,344m. This can also equate to three hundred hours of competitive football—that's more than three full soccer matches in a row or a rowing session of six hours.

Babies are born with kneecaps that don't start to turn bony (ossify) until three years of age. Before that they are made of cartilage (Dr. Heba Ismail, Pediatrician).

Three children will use approximately 24,638 disposable diapers. It will take between 200–460 years for those disposable diapers to decompose amounting to 7.5 tons of trash (US EPA).

SUCCESS

You can use most any measure
When you're speaking of success.

You can measure it in fancy homes,
Expensive cars, and dress.

But the measure of your real success
Is the one you cannot spend.

It's the way your kids describe you
When they're talking to a friend.

—*Martin Buxbaum*

*Shared by Amy Iverson-Phillips

AFTERWORD

Blythe Lipman has done it again, creating another useful book for parents. In her first book, *Help! My Baby Came Without Instructions*, she provided practical tips for new parents to help them get through that first year and make it a little easier. Now she has extended her practical advice and created an easy-to-use parent advice book about toddlers. Blythe uses a light touch, emphasizes the many options available, and provides useful norms for children, including potty-training age, how many hours toddlers should be sleeping, and so much more. I highly recommend this book for parents of toddlers. It will help them get through this potentially stressful period with understanding and fun.

I have known Blythe for over ten years. She's a parent, educator, author, and baby and toddler expert who has helped some of my more anxious families with babies struggling with nap and sleep issues. Blythe is a popular speaker at parent education workshops, combining her wisdom and experience with scientific knowledge to make those toddler years a breeze.

Besides your pediatrician, parents of infants and toddlers should consider having Blythe's book along for the ride. Enjoy your toddler!

Ron Fischler, MD
North Scottsdale Pediatrics
Scottsdale, Arizona

ABOUT THE AUTHOR

BLYTHE LIPMAN is the president and founder of Baby Instructions, headquartered in Arizona. She is passionate about babies, toddlers, and their parents. Blythe has worked in the field for thirty-five years. She is an experienced baby and toddler expert and parent educator with a national following.

Blythe has been the "CEO" (Lead Teacher) of many infant and toddler rooms in preschools throughout the country as well as a consultant setting up turn-key operations, designing and creating innovative infant and toddler rooms that provide a homey yet stimulating atmosphere that allows each child to achieve their milestones. She writes the parent manuals, daily report sheets, parent data forms, as well as teacher contracts, instruction books, and provides on-site teacher training.

She works extensively with parents on an individual basis and has been a presenter at many national educator conferences as well as serving on the Prevent Child Abuse Arizona Task Force. She writes articles for many publications as well as weekly blog posts on www.babyinstructions.com.

Blythe is featured on numerous television and radio shows throughout the country and in Canada, sharing her easy-to-use tips and expertise with over a million viewers. Blythe hosts a weekly Internet radio show called *Baby and Toddler Instructions*, on www.Toginet.com each Wednesday, as well as doing a monthly parenting segment on *Arizona Midday* KPNX (NBC Affiliate).

Blythe lives in Arizona with her two puppies, Lucy and Desi, and has two grown children.

To contact Blythe and receive free monthly tips, send your email address to babyinstructions@cox.net.

Take a peek at her website: www.babyinstructions.com. She would love to hear from you!

SELECTED BIBLIOGRAPHY

Debroff, Stacy M. *The Mom Book: 4,278 of Mom Central's Tips…for Moms, from Moms.* New York: The Free Press, 2002.

Douglas, Ann. *The Mother of All Toddler Books: An All-Canadian Guide to Your Child's Second and Third Years.* New York: Wiley Publishing Inc., 2004.

Fields, Denise and Ari Brown. *Toddler 411: Clear Answers and Smart Advice for Your Toddler.* Boulder, CO: Windsor Peak Press, 2011.

Murkoff, Heidi, Arlene Eisenberg, and Sandee Hathaway. *What to Expect: The Toddler Years.* New York: Workman Books, 2009.

Singer, Jen. *Stop Second-Guessing Yourself: The Toddler Years.* Deerfield Beach, FL: Health Communications, Inc., 2009.

TO OUR READERS

Viva Editions publishes books that inform, enlighten, and entertain. We do our best to bring you, the reader, quality books that celebrate life, inspire the mind, revive the spirit, and enhance lives all around. Our authors are practical visionaries: people who offer deep wisdom in a hopeful and helpful manner. Viva was launched with an attitude of growth and we want to spread our joy and offer our support and advice where we can to help you live the Viva way: vivaciously!

We're grateful for all our readers and want to keep bringing you books for inspired living. We invite you to write to us with your comments and suggestions, and what you'd like to see more of. You can also sign up for our online newsletter to learn about new titles, author events, and special offers.

Viva Editions
2246 Sixth St.
Berkeley, CA 94710
www.vivaeditions.com
(800) 780-2279
Follow us on Twitter @vivaeditions
Friend/fan us on Facebook